HOLY MARY

GETTING TO KNOW AND LOVE OUR BLESSED MOTHER THROUGH HER MAGNIFICENT TITLES

THE VERY REV. CORNELIUS JOSEPH O'CONNELL

JOHN MURPHY COMPANY
Publishers
300 W. Lombard Street, Baltimore, Maryland

America Needs Fatima
P.O. Box 341, Hanover, PA 17331
(888) 317-5571
ANF@ANF.org • www.ANF.org

B81

To order more copies of this book, contact:

U.S.A. **$8.95**
America Needs Fatima
(888) 317-5571
P.O. Box 341, Hanover, PA 17331
www.ANF.org
ANF@ANF.org

Canada *Free*
Canada Needs Our Lady
P.O. Box 36040, Greenfield Park, QC J4V 3N7
1-844-729-6279 (1-844-Say-Mary)
www.CanadaNeedsOurLady.org
Info@CanadaNeedsOurLady.org

Cover design: Svetlana Uscumlic
Book design: Marie Jordan
Copy editors: Tonia Long and Anne Drake
The title of this edition is our own. The original title is *The Life of the Blessed Virgin Mary, As Set Forth in Her Litany*. The current edition was edited and adjusted for the benefit of the modern reader.

ISBN: 9781877905483
Library of Congress Control Number: 2016941640

CONTENTS

©iStockphoto.com/Arpand Benedek

PREFACE

Every child loves his mother unconditionally. His heart's devotion finds its expression not only in words, but in an untiring display of little feats and accomplishments. With each new day, he finds creative ways to impress on his mother how much he not only loves her, but how deeply he treasures her and desires her approval.

Children never tire of repeating the praises of their mother. They cherish the tenderest affection for her, whose loveliness is ever present before their eyes. In the home, they gather around her. When absent, they think of her and long to return to her gentle smile and loving embrace.

In their appreciation of her, she is the best, the fairest, the greatest, yes, the noblest, the most lovable, the most beautiful of all women. There is none comparable to her. She surpasses all others. They brag about her to their playmates, and resent the slightest criticism of her. Their life is entirely wrapped up in hers.

As devoted children of the Blessed Virgin Mary, it was our love for this incomparable Mother which caused us to write this book in her honor. And it is at the feet of this most admirable of mothers that we desire to lay our deed of homage.

Even if every one of her children wrote a book, extolling her graces, there would still remain much more to be written in her honor. We cannot sing her praises too joyously, nor too often. The more we publish her perfections, her purity, her chastity, the more reason we will find to praise her many other virtues.

God has raised her so far above all His creatures, that what all men, and even all nations, might do to make her name greater would be, in comparison to His love for her, less than a raindrop compared to the waters of all the rivers and oceans of the world combined.

If these pages will help even one mind know her better, one heart love her more, or one more soul sing her praises, I shall deem my humble efforts well repaid.

In writing this book about the Virgin Mother of our Redeemer, our own dear Mother, my soul's desire is to draw others to be her devout clients. They will stand with all the saints and angels of God, proving by their praises the truth of her glorious prophecy: "All generations shall call me blessed" (Luke 1:48).

CHAPTER I
Holy Mary

Sanctity can be summed up as follows: to cultivate a constant friendship and a sincere love for God; to seek the companionship of Jesus; to turn our mind and heart from worldly concerns; to avoid evil and to do good.

Holiness of life is gained by faithfully doing one's duty and practicing virtue. Saint Paul tells us what we must do to live such a life when he says: "Denying ungodliness and worldly desires, we should live soberly, and justly, and godly in this world" (Titus 2:12).

To sanctify the body, one must practice purity. The practice of humility and charity will sanctify the soul, as illustrated by the following Scripture quotes:

"I beseech you, brethren, by the mercy of God, that you present your bodies, a living sacrifice, holy, pleasing unto God" (Rom. 12:1).

Jesus Christ sanctified His Church, "that He might present it to Himself, a glorious church, not having spot or wrinkle, or any such thing; but that it should be holy, and without blemish" (Eph. 5:27).

"For to me, to live" says Saint Paul, "is Christ" (Phil. 1:21). "And I live, now not I, but Christ lives in me" (Gal. 2:20).

Our life must be, as far as possible, a counterpart of the life of our Savior. We must not be ashamed of Him; we must take up our cross and follow Him; we must die for love of Him, die to all things earthly. In a word, we must seek to be another Christ.

The measure of a holy life lies in the conformity of our will and of our works to the eternal law, which is in the spirit of God. He who regulates his ways, in accordance with that law, is just, holy, perfect.

Sanctity is freedom from all blemish. It is a true love of God, an intimate union with Christ. The more we turn our heart away and purify it from worldly things, the nearer we approach to God, and the more holy do we become.

"Blessed be the God and Father of our Lord Jesus Christ," says the Apostle, "Who hath blessed us with spiritual blessings in heavenly places, in Christ. As He chose us in Him before the foundation of the world, that we should be holy and unspotted in His sight in charity" (Eph. 1:3-4).

God alone is sanctity in His essence, He is eternal charity. Whoever seeks a union with God, and converses with Him, lives a life pleasing to Him. Our sanctity increases the closer we get to God and the more our devotion to Him grows.

The humble Virgin of Nazareth, Mary, being the nearest and most intimately united to God, is, of all His creatures, the most holy. A closer union with God never existed, nor could a more perfect union exist than that which resulted from her role as the Mother of God.

Notwithstanding Mary's close relationship with God as His Mother, it would have done little to increase her sanctity if she had not carried Jesus Christ in her heart, even more than in her chaste womb.

All her life, Mary ignored the things of this world, abhorred sin, and lived only for Jesus. All her days were passed in the practice of virtue. With greater reason than Saint Paul could she exclaim: "And I live, now not I, but Christ lives in me" (Gal. 2:20).

She was holy in the use of her five senses; she was godly in all of her thoughts, desires, words, and in all the powers of her soul; she was saintly in all her movements, all her actions; in a word, she was holy in both body and soul.

Jesus was, by nature, without sin. Mary, preserved by a special privilege of divine grace from the stain of original sin, was exempt from any actual stain, even from the least imperfection.

Jesus dwelt in Mary's immaculate womb for nine months, was nourished at her breasts in infancy, and spent thirty of the thirty-three years of His life under her roof.

Mary took part in His labors and shared in His joys and sorrows. From the moment of her conception, a most splendid beauty graced her pure soul. In her infancy she consecrated herself to God, Whom she loved with an affection beyond that of all creatures capable of serving Him. She had no thought, no desire, save that of honoring Him. She performed no duty nor undertook any task unless it would serve His greater glory. Her mind was in perfect harmony with His mind; her heart pulsated only in union with that of her Savior; her soul was filled with joyous rapture in her ecstasy of devotion to Him. Never for one moment in her life did she displease Him in thought, word or deed.

She knew not evil; no shadow of sin ever clouded her life, no stain of any kind ever darkened her soul.

She not only lived, but died for love of God, for it was her desire to be with Him that caused her soul to wing its flight to the sweet embrace of her divine Son, Jesus.

Like Him, she was tried. Nevertheless, her sorrows drew her closer to God, to Whom she had recourse for help and consolation. In the spirit of her divine Son, Who exclaimed, "Not what I will, but what Thou wilt" (Mark 14:36), she humbly submitted to God's holy will in these words: "Behold the handmaid of the Lord; be it done to me according to Thy word" (Luke 1:38).

Even though Mary did not fully understand the words Simeon said to her concerning her divine Son, her love for, and confidence in, her Maker was such that her heart was transfixed with a sword of sorrow. Her mind and heart were at all times one with that of God. "Be it done to me according to Thy word," came forth every moment from her pure and holy soul.

She was humble, like the meek and humble Jesus, and the Lord "hath regarded the humility of His handmaid" (Luke 1:48). Her devotion for Jesus was like that of Saint Peter; her charity, like that of Saint John; her obedience, like that of Abraham; her patience, like that of Isaac; her submission, like that of Jacob; her purity exceeded that of all the angels and saints; her constancy was like that of Joshua; her goodness, like that of Samuel; her tenderness, like that of David; and her abstinence, like that of Daniel.

Responding faithfully to every requirement of a perfect life, she is indeed that Holy Mary of whom it is said in the Holy Scriptures: "Hail, full of grace, the Lord is with thee, blessed art thou among women" (Luke 1:28).

CHAPTER II
Holy Mother of God

"Blessed are the eyes that see the things which you see" (Luke 10:23). These words were spoken by Jesus to His disciples, so they might understand how privileged they were to believe He was the Messiah promised to the Patriarchs and Prophets. They were blessed to accept His teachings, as He unfolded to them the secrets of His Father and the eternal truths of heaven.

We can address these same words, "blessed are the eyes that see the things which you see," to the children of the household of the faith, who acknowledge holy Mary to be the Mother of God, seeing as they do the truth of this sublime mystery.

One day our Lord asked His Apostles: "Whom do men say that the Son of Man is? But they said: Some John the Baptist, and others, Elias, and others, Jeremias, or one of the prophets. Jesus said to them: But whom do you say that I am? Simon Peter answered and said: Thou art Christ, the Son of the Living God. And Jesus answering, said to him: Blessed art thou, Simon Bar-Jona, because flesh and blood has not revealed it to thee, but My Father who is in Heaven" (Matt. 16:13-17).

This question may be put to the world today, in regard to Holy Mary: "Whom do men say that she is?" And the answer comes: some, an ordinary woman, and others, a good woman, and others, "man's tainted nature's solitary boast."

But whom do *you* say that she is? And the child of faith responds: "She is the Holy Mother of God." Flesh and blood did not reveal it to you, but our Father Who is in Heaven. "Bless-

The Virgin Mary became the Mother of God the instant she responded to the Archangel Gabriel with the words: "Behold the handmaid of the Lord; be it done to me according to thy word" (Luke 1:38). Painting by Dias Tavares.

ed are the eyes that see the things that you see."

It is by the unerring eye of faith that we believe Mary to be the holy Mother of God.

No man will disown his own mother. To him she is the best, the greatest, the loveliest of women. And yet, though she be the mother of his body, she is not the mother of his soul, for God Himself breathes the soul into every man born into the world.

Mary, although one of God's creatures like ourselves, is His holy Mother. While she is not the Mother of the God-head, she is the Mother of the Word made flesh, Who is God, equal to the Father from all eternity. Hence, she is truly the Mother of God.

When you proclaim your faith in the Incarnation, in the same breath you affirm that Mary is the Mother of God. In the Incarnation, God takes unto Himself a human nature, remaining always God. Therefore, He is perfect Man, as well as true God.

But in His human nature, He is truly the Son of the Blessed Virgin Mary. From her most chaste womb He took that flesh and blood, whereby He became man. The relationship, therefore, between God, as to His human nature, and Mary is the same as that between any mother and her son.

While firmly proclaiming this intimate union between God and the Blessed Virgin, we also declare that she is not the Mother of God in His *divine* nature, for in this He is her Creator. She is none the less His holy Mother, in His *human* nature, for this human nature is the human nature of God, of which she is the Mother. Mary is, therefore, in very deed, the holy Mother of God, since from her the Eternal Son of God borrowed His flesh and blood and became man.

It was this Divine Person, our Lord Jesus Christ, Who, by the power of the Holy Ghost, was conceived in her virginal womb and was born of her. Through this indescribable mystery of the Incarnation of the Son of God, Mary holds a unique place in the plan of man's redemption and salvation. For God has chosen to redeem us in His human nature, and not in His divine nature—in that nature, therefore, which He took from His holy Mother, Mary.

In this, God has honored and exalted her above all other creatures, having endowed her with all the beauty and graces a creature is capable of receiving.

Our great love and devotion for Mary, the holy Mother of God, springs from her relationship with God. This keeps alive in our hearts the great mystery of a God becoming man, through Whom every blessing of Heaven comes to us. We honor Mary as the holy Mother of God, for God Himself so honors her, having chosen her from all eternity to be His Mother.

No higher dignity could the Creator give to His creature, than the one He bestowed upon Mary, the humble handmaid of the Lord. We would fail in our duty to God if we did not give to His holy Mother the respect and honor that she deserves.

Who does not love his mother above all others? Who would not shed his last drop of blood for her sake? Is God to be eclipsed by His own creatures in the veneration that a mother receives from her child? God's love for Mary tells us no. He favored her above all women, when He bestowed upon her from the first moment of her conception, an incomparable beauty of both body and soul. With quiet satisfaction did He look upon her, and with a child's love and devotion for His Mother, has Jesus at all times honored her as His holy Mother.

Mary is also our Mother. Every true child of the Church considers himself blessed in being able to call her his holy Mother. She is not, it is true, our natural mother. But she is our spiritual Mother, since she gave voluntarily her chaste womb to be the sanctuary of the Son of God, Jesus Christ. Through Him we have been redeemed and brought to a higher and better life, the spiritual life in Christ Jesus.

All who accept the mystery of the Incarnation of the Son of God, must recognize this spiritual relationship between Mary, the Mother of Jesus Christ, and those ransomed through His precious blood, shed for them on Calvary.

As her loving children, let us honor her as God honors her; let us love her as He loves her; let us magnify her name on earth, as the blessed do in Heaven. Let us call upon her as our most sweet, most loving Mother Mary. May we be privileged to mingle our praises with those of all the angels and saints in Heaven, to honor her as God Himself honors her, as His holy Mother and ours, through Jesus Christ.

CHAPTER III
Holy Virgin of Virgins

"Blessed art thou among women" (Luke 1:28). Mary, ever virgin, is the most blessed among all women. Over seven hundred years before her birth, the prophet Isaiah announced: "Behold a Virgin shall conceive and bear a Son, and His name shall be called Emmanuel" (7:14). The angel Gabriel confirmed: "He shall be great, and shall be called the Son of the Most High; and the Lord God shall give unto Him the throne of David His father; and He shall reign in the house of Jacob forever. And of His kingdom there shall be no end" (Luke 1:32, 33).

In God's own time, He sent the Angel Gabriel to the Virgin Mary to announce to her that she would conceive in her womb and bring forth a Son. "How shall I become a mother," said Mary to the angel, "for I have consecrated myself to God; I have taken a vow of virginity; I wish to continue faithful to my promises; I am a virgin, and I desire to remain a virgin!"

How Mary treasured her virginity! How she cherished the beauty of her pure soul! She preferred the loveliness of her most chaste heart to the honors she would receive if she were to become the Mother of God.

Mary was the first of all women to consecrate her virginity to God. Not bound by any law or following the example of one who had gone before her, she made the offering of herself to the Almighty, and in so doing, became the Virgin of Virgins. Now countless virgin souls, following her example, take it upon themselves to live in this holy, happy, and exalted state.

It was only on the condition that she would remain a

virgin that Mary agreed to become the Mother of the Savior. The angel assured her that she would remain a virgin always, for: "The Holy Ghost shall come upon thee, and the power of the Most High shall overshadow thee. And therefore also the Holy One who shall be born of thee shall be called the Son of God" (Luke 1:35).

With the assurance that she would not lose her virginity, the Virgin of Virgins exclaimed: "Behold the handmaid of the Lord; be it done to me according to thy word" (Luke 1:38). Mary conceived and brought forth a Son, without the loss of her virginity. Jesus Christ, the Redeemer, honored Mary's virginity and in so doing enabled her purity to eclipse that of the Angels.

Along with the woman in the Song of Songs, Mary proclaims, "I am the flower of the field, and the lily of the valleys" (Cant. 2:1).

Of her, it is also said, "She is a vapor of the power of God, and a certain pure emanation of the glory of the Almighty God: and, therefore, no defiled thing will come into her." (Wisd. 7:25)

"For she is the brightness of eternal light, and the unspotted mirror of God's majesty, and the image of His goodness" (Wisd. 7:26).

For she is the Immaculate Conception. She is without spot, the fairest flower of the field, the whitest and purest lily of the valleys.

This is the Virgin spoken of by the Prophets, whose beauty of body and soul dims the loveliness and purity of the brightest angels. She is the Virgin before whom the Archangel Gabriel prostrated himself. She is that Virgin of Virgins whom all generations shall call blessed.

CHAPTER IV
Mother of Christ

Before God banished Adam and Eve from the Garden of Eden, and by their toils and trials bade them earn their livelihood, He promised to them a Savior. In His eternal design, this same Savior was none other than His own beloved Son, Jesus.

It is He Who should crush the head of the serpent, whose malice brought sin into the world. This Savior of men will be of the seed of the woman, and will take to Himself her flesh and blood. He will dwell in her chaste womb, as in a tabernacle. He is called Christ: "Thou art the Christ, the Son of the living God" (Matt. 16:16). Mary is, therefore, His Mother, for He was conceived of the Holy Ghost in her virginal womb, took for His Flesh her flesh and blood, and was born of her. Albeit true God, He is true man also, formed in the womb of the Virgin Mary.

Between Christ and Mary exists the very real relationship of Son and Mother. Mary is His Mother; Jesus is her Son. He was, in His humanity, subject to the Blessed Virgin, as every good son loves and is obedient to his mother. "He went down [...] to Nazareth, and was subject to them" (Luke 2:51). Christ loved His Mother tenderly while on earth, and loves her now devotedly in Heaven.

The first public miracle performed by Jesus, the first manifestation of His Divine power, was in obedience to the wish of His Mother, at the marriage feast of Cana, when He changed the water into wine.

His last public act of kindness occurred after His cruel, bitter passion, after His trying journey to Mount Calvary, after being nailed to the gibbet of the cross. Even in the very throes of death, the loving heart of the Child went out to His Mother, whom He sees sorrowful beneath His Cross, and He asked His beloved Apostle, Saint John, to care for her, and take her as his own mother.

Only after He had provided for the best, the greatest and dearest of His treasures on earth, His Mother, was Christ prepared to give up His spirit into the hands of His Heavenly Father for our redemption. Bowing, therefore, His head, he spoke the words: "It is consummated," and died.

"What more can I do than give my life for you." These words of Christ are especially applicable to His Mother Mary, for while it is true that He died for the redemption of all men, it was through the anticipated merits of His holy passion and death that His Mother, Mary, was conceived without sin. And it was through her Immaculate Conception that she was thus made worthy of the sublime dignity to which she was called.

The relationship between Christ and Mary, as Son and Mother, exists now, though both are in the Kingdom of Heaven, as well as it did while they lived on earth.

In the world Christ obeyed and loved her, and He still gives her this same obedience and love in Heaven. His child-like affection for her never wanes. His respect for her is that of a devoted Son, while His love for her is greater than for all the blessed in Heaven.

Knowing this, we should be filled with confidence when we appeal to the Mother of Christ, our life, our sweetness and our hope. She will pray and intercede for us, at the throne of her Divine Son, for Christ will not turn a deaf ear to the pleas of His Mother, the ever spotless Blessed Virgin Mary.

CHAPTER V
Mother of Divine Grace

Jesus is the source of every grace that comes to us from the throne of mercy. Through Him all of Heaven's blessings are given to us. From His Sacred Heart flowed His life's blood, as an offering acceptable to His Heavenly Father. This perfect offering satisfied His just anger and caused Him to throw wide open the gates of divine grace and rain down His choicest favors upon mankind.

Our Redeemer paid a great price for those heavenly favors. He left the bosom of His Father, became man and sojourned among men for thirty-three years. He shared in their labors, participated in their sufferings, and died upon the cross, to merit for them redemption and everlasting life.

All happiness and all graces come to us through Him. But Mary is the Mother of Jesus Christ. Therefore, it is right and good to call her the "Mother of Divine Grace."

Is it any wonder, then, that the Angel Gabriel should salute her: "Hail, full of grace, the Lord is with thee" (Luke 1:28)? Mary abounds in grace, she is a veritable ocean of graces. As the waters of all the rivers are swallowed up in those of the sea, so the graces of the Angels, Patriarchs, Prophets, Apostles, Martyrs, Confessors, Virgins and of all the Saints are centered in Mary, "full of grace."

"The Most High has sanctified His own tabernacle" (Ps. 45:5). His Mother is that tabernacle. The Word was made flesh in her womb; the body of Jesus Christ was formed out of the substance of the Most Blessed Virgin Mary, and this dignity necessarily entitled her to the fullness of all graces.

"In Him (Christ) dwells all the fullness of the Godhead

corporally" (Col. 2:9). But Christ took up His abode in Mary, hence the fullness of His divinity was in her, and with it the abundance of grace, so that when she became the Mother of Christ, she became the Mother of Divine Grace.

Mary surpasses the greatness of the whole world, for He, whom the world cannot contain, was conceived in her. She alone eclipses the vastness of the heavens, since she gave a home to Him, Whom the heavens are unable to hold. The fountains of grace that enhance the souls of the saints, making them holy before God, have their source in Mary.

Of her, it is written in the Holy Scriptures: "I was exalted like a cedar in Libanus, and as a cypress tree on Mount Sion. I was exalted like a palm tree in Cades, and as a rose plant in Jericho. As a fair olive tree in the plains, and as a plane tree by the water in the streets, was I exalted. I gave a sweet smell like cinnamon, and aromatical balm. I yielded a sweet odor like the best myrrh. And I perfumed my dwelling as storax and galbanum, and onyx, and aloes, and as the frank-incense not cut, and my odor is as the purest balm.

"I have stretched out my branches as the turpentine tree, and my branches are of honor and grace. As the vine, I have brought forth a pleasant odor, and my flowers are the fruit of honor and riches. I am the mother of fair love, and of fear, and of knowledge, and of holy hope. In me is all grace of the way, and of the truth, in me is all hope of life and of virtue" (Ecclus. 24:17-25).

All that is here written by the inspired writer and applied to Mary, the Mother of our Lord, portrays in beautiful language her eminent sanctity, exalted virtue, and the fullness of grace that adorns her soul.

While Christ is the way, Mary, Mother of Divine Grace, leads us to it. Though He is the truth, she, who is full of wis-

Statue of Our Lady of Graces at the America Needs Fatima headquarters, Spring Grove, Pennsylvania.

dom, guides us in the way of truth. And, while He is full of life, in her is all hope of life and of virtue.

What we are, we are by the grace of God. Of ourselves we can do nothing worthy of life eternal. We are worthy of God's grace through the merits of Christ. But Mary is the Mother of Christ, and as such the Mother of Divine Grace, for every grace from Heaven comes to us through Jesus Christ, her Divine Son.

CHAPTER VI
Mother Most Pure

Mary, though a mother, remained always a virgin. The laws of nature were suspended in her regard. She conceived and gave birth to a son, the Son of God, yet still she remained a virgin without spot or stain in her. It was fitting that her purity should be the greatest after that of Jesus, her Divine Son.

It was befitting her dignity as the Mother of God that she should shine forth in purity of both body and soul, unequalled by angel or saint. Applying the words of the Book of Wisdom, she is called "a vapor of the power of God, and a certain pure emanation of the glory of the Almighty God: and, therefore, no defiled thing will come into her" (7:25).

Because of her great purity, Mary has been likened to the dove, the holy Jerusalem, the sublime throne of God, the ark of sanctification and the house built by Eternal Wisdom.

She is spoken of as the queen filled with delights, resting upon her beloved, and who came from the mouth of the Most High all perfect, all beautiful, all pure in His sight.

For this reason did God greet her in the words of the Archangel, "Hail, full of grace." The same reason prompted Saint Elizabeth to greet her, "Blessed art thou among women." She is blessed among women because of her incomparable purity of body and soul, whereby she outranks all the saints and angels.

So pure is Mary that she became disturbed at the presence even of an angel. When the messenger of God announced to her that she was chosen to become the Mother of God, she hesitated, and would have declined the honor, had it entailed the loss of her virginal purity, which she prized above all honors.

Saint Paul, in his Epistle to the Romans, urges the faithful to keep their bodies pure. "I beseech you, by the mercy of God that you present your bodies as a living sacrifice, holy, pleasing unto God. And be not conformed to this world; but be reformed in the newness of your mind, that you may prove what is the good, and the acceptable, and the perfect will of God" (Rom. 12:1, 2).

He will have us to offer our bodies to God, and to make them worthy to love and honor Him. As a "living sacrifice," our bodies must be pure and free from all stain or blemish.

"Know you not," says

Statue of the Mother of God, Westminster Abbey, London, England.

the same Apostle, "that your members are the temple of the Holy Ghost, who is in you, whom you have from God; and you are not your own? For you are bought with a great price. Glorify and bear God in your body" (1 Cor. 6:19-20).

Mary, of all women, is the only one who so bore God in her body. She gave of her body the material to frame a body for Christ, so that He might become man. Her body was truly sanctified, for there was no blemish in it, but it was a veritable vessel of honor, a body all holy, all pure.

"Blessed," said our Lord, "are the clean of heart for they shall see God" (Matt. 5:8). They shall see God here by His grace. In Heaven, they will see Him through the beatific vision, possessing and enjoying eternal glory.

Mary is "full of grace," hence the most pure. Even now she is blessed with the beatific vision and eternal glory, the reward of those who die in the Lord. It is fitting that she should possess God for all eternity because she is His most pure Mother.

As no defilement ever marred the perfection of either her body or her soul, it is her right and privilege that her body should not turn to dust, but be with her most pure soul in the kingdom of her divine Son.

No wonder, then, that we firmly believe with the Doctors and Fathers of the Church in the assumption of Mary into the kingdom of Heaven.

CHAPTER VII
Mother Most Chaste

To be chaste is to be angelic. What is there more beautiful, or more excellent than chastity which makes men pure like the angels?

Chastity represents in the world the glorious state of immortality. It requires no ornament outside of itself, being its own most beautiful adornment. It makes us pleasing to God, unites us with Jesus Christ, combats the malicious tendencies of the flesh, gives peace to the body, and, possessing in its essence unimaginable joy, it renders all who enjoy it perfectly happy.

It is a shield to our eyes. It dispels darkness and creates brightness. Chastity reins in the flesh and directs it heavenward. It fills the heart with delight and furnishes wings to the soul whereon it may soar to the throne of God.

It gives spiritual joy and overcomes sorrow. It curbs the violence of our passions, weakens our inclination to sin and frees the soul from the relentless attacks of the flesh.

We may apply to this great virtue the words of Wisdom: "All gold, in comparison of her, is as a little sand; and silver, in respect to her, shall be counted as clay" (7:9). And again: "Love her above health and beauty, and choose to have her instead of light: for her light cannot be put out" (7:10).

"For she is more beautiful than the sun and above all the order of the stars: being compared with the light, she is found before it" (Wisd. 7:29).

Chastity ennobles and glorifies whoever possesses it. Do you desire great riches? What is more precious than chastity?

She should be our closest companion in life, having the

promise that through the practice of this virtue we will one day enjoy the greatest wealth. In our cares and sorrows, she will be our sweetest comfort. Through the practice of chastity, we shall win everlasting life and leave for those who come after us a steadfast memory.

In our home she shall be company to us. Her speech being pure, she shall be a source of joy and gladness to us.

Unless God grant us the grace to do so, we cannot practice chastity. With humble and loving hearts we should seek it at His merciful hands.

"He that is mighty," may the chaste soul exclaim with Mary, "has done great things to me" (Luke 1:49). "He has showed might in His arm" (Luke 1:51).

The beautiful descriptions of Judas Maccabees in the Scriptures also apply most admirably to those who practice the virtue of chastity:

"He put on a breastplate as a giant, and girt his warlike armor about him in battles, and protected the camp with his sword. In his acts he was like a lion, and like a lion's whelp roaring for his prey. And he pursued the wicked and sought them out [...] and all the workers of iniquity were troubled; and salvation prospered in his hand. And he [...] made Jacob glad with his works, and his memory is blessed forever" (1 Macc. 3-7).

It was by his chastity that the youthful Joseph of the Old Testament gave evidence of his great valor. His mantle was seized by the hand of an evil woman, but his mind and heart remained free. He relinquished his garment, but clung to his purity.

"Know you not, that you are the temple of God, and that the Spirit of God dwells in you?" (1 Cor. 3:16).The Apostle Saint Paul tells us to keep ourselves pure because we are the temple of God. If this can be said of us poor sinners, what can be said of Mary, the Immaculate, who carried God Himself in her chaste womb?

We are the temple, not of man, but of God. We are a holy temple, a temple wherein God loves to dwell, especially when it is adorned with chastity. "But if any man violate the temple of God, him shall God destroy. For the temple of God is holy, which you are" (1 Cor. 3:17).

Of all the children of men, Mary is the holiest, the fairest, the purest. None of God's creatures, whether in the heavens or on the earth, can come close to matching her beauty or her loveliness.

She is His temple, undefiled, and three-times holy:

—by her eminent sanctity and grace with which the Father endowed her;

—by the overshadowing of the Holy Ghost, Who chose her as His chaste spouse;

—and in conceiving in her immaculate womb Jesus Christ, the beloved Son of the Father, and her own Divine Son.

Eternal holiness, infinite chastity, God the all-perfect, chose her as His mother, the mother of Jesus, the infinite source of all grace.

It was among the pure, white lilies of her virginal womb that He took up His abode among men. She was all fair in His sight, and He rejoiced in the beauty of her chaste body and soul. Full of grace, she was pre-eminently holy and pure. Because of her perfect chastity, He made use of her immaculate flesh and blood to become her Son, without the least offense to her chastity. For she remained always a virgin, while becoming Mother Most Chaste of Jesus, the Son of God and the Redeemer of mankind.

CHAPTER VIII
Mother Undefiled

"Man's life is a warfare" (Job 7:1) here below, not merely for a time, but throughout its whole course. On every side the powers of darkness conspire against us. The seductions of a wicked world and the temptations of the flesh seem intent on drawing us away from union with God.

While every man is born with the guilt of sin upon him, his soul is made as white as the purest fleece by the cleansing waters of holy baptism. From a child stained with original sin he becomes a child of God.

Through the efficacy of the regenerating waters of baptism, we are made pleasing in the sight of God, since there is no longer a stain upon us. Hence our Lord said, "Suffer the little children, and forbid them not, to come to me: for the kingdom of Heaven is for such" (Matt. 19:14).

But how short-lived, for most men, is the holy innocence of their childhood! Are we not told in Holy Scripture that he that says he does no wrong is a liar?

Nature offers many examples of how quickly purity gives way to impurity. The resplendent rays of the sun are obscured by darkness, often by ominous clouds. The snowflakes that cover the earth with a pure white blanket are quickly dirtied when coming in contact with the earth. Like the pure sparkling waters, gurgling forth from the depths of the earth that are soon muddied in their course, is the life of man on his journey to his final goal.

All that glitters is not gold, and much, very much, of what there is in the world is like the fruit of the Dead Sea—that is, beautiful to behold, yet crumbles to dust at your touch. So it is with the lives of many men. Some show great promise and virtue in their youth. But then their sworn enemy, the foul spirit of darkness, steals into their hearts and robs them of their innocence.

Others, like a gently flowing stream of crystalline water, move along serenely and gently. But then they get deflected from their natural course and are drawn into a polluted channel through the alluring promises of a wicked world. While others still, like the giant tree of the forest, or the rosy fruit of the orchard, contain veiled in their core a worm that gnaws away at them from the inside until they decay and fall to the ground.

Is there, then, no one to be found among the children of men whom God made to His own image and likeness, who has not fallen prey to temptation, to the fascinations of a corrupt world, or to the trials of the flesh?

There is one, and only one, our own sweet, loving, humble Mother Mary, the Mother of our Savior. Like the sweet violet, nestled in the shadows of the hillside, hidden, yet filling the air with its delicate perfume, do we find the handmaid of the Lord. She gives forth the most exquisite aroma of incomparable virtues, this humble Virgin of Nazareth, the Mother of God and our most sweet and loving Mother Undefiled.

It is an article of our Faith that at no time in all the course of her existence, from the very instant of her Immaculate Conception to the close of her most pure life, did the slightest stain tarnish her immaculate soul or her most chaste body. Nothing marred their loveliness before Him Who is infinite sanctity, her Creator.

She is all fair, all beautiful and as radiant as the rising sun, spotless as the sunbeam, white as the snowflake, without spot or stain, free from the blight that overtook man in paradise.

She is the spotless virgin of virgins, the Mother of Jesus, His Mother Undefiled.

CHAPTER IX
Mother Untouched

Imagine a farmer who grows fruit trees. His greatest ambition is to possess a beautiful orchard with all kinds of fruit-bearing trees. To accomplish this, he first invests a great deal of time and effort in carefully selecting land suited to his project, then he turns his attention to the trees to be planted, the fertilizers to be used, and all the tools necessary for the work of properly tilling the land.

Having made the choice of a field he considers best suited for his purpose, he begins to prepare the ground for planting his trees.

He plows and replows the soil, he fertilizes it well, harrows and rolls it and spaces it off. He looks after the work himself and sees that all is well done. He then proceeds to choose the fruit trees he desires to plant and he supervises their planting in keeping with his fixed plan.

After some years of tireless care, cultivating and irrigating the orchard, pruning the trees in due season, he finds that his labors are about to be crowned with an abundant crop of the most delicate and savory fruit.

Day after day he goes into his orchard, examines the trees, the leaves, and the ripening fruit and sees that all is good.

His heart rejoices over the splendid prospect. His eyes feast on the wonderful picture his orchard presents. Soon, very soon, the rosy, the yellow, the pink, the white colored fruits of various kinds will be gathered in and his soul will overflow with gladness.

At last the day is appointed when he, with his employees, will begin to gather the fruit. But, the night before this long-awaited day, a violent wind storm passes over the section of the country wherein his orchard is located, bearing, as on wings, millions upon millions of insects that settle on every tree and fruit in his orchard.

The next morning, when he and his laborers set about their work, they find every tree damaged, every fruit tainted. Every tree except one lone tree with its fruit. This tree he had placed at the base of a high knoll, which sheltered it from the wind.

This was the only tree, and its luscious fruit the only fruit, untouched by the plague of insects that swarmed upon all the others in the orchard.

Though saddened at the blight that had come upon his work, the farmer was not broken in spirit. From the tree that remained untouched and had escaped ruin he was able to replant a second orchard, without which his labors would have been entirely fruitless.

Is not this farmer and his work like God and the work of His creation?

He made the heavens and the earth. He embellished the heavens with lights to divide the day and the night, to be for signs and for seasons, and for days and for years.

In the firmament He placed a greater luminary to rule the day, and a lesser light and the stars He made to govern the night. They were all intended to dispel darkness and light up the world.

He had the earth bring forth green herbs, fruit-bearing plants, and trees of every kind. He planted a paradise of pleasure, and in it brought forth all manner of trees beautiful to behold and whose fruit was most delightful to eat.

Seeing that all was done as He willed, He created man, forming him of the clay of the earth, and breathed into him a living soul. To His own image and likeness did God make man, and placed him in the garden of delights with power to rule over His creation.

"Of every tree of paradise you shall eat," said the Lord

God to man, "but of the tree of knowledge of good and evil, you shall not eat. For on the day you shall eat of it, you shall die" (Gen. 2:16-17).

We know the rest of the story. There came a day, a fatal day for man, when the spirit of darkness, the enemy of both God and man, entered the garden of paradise. By cunning speech he convinced man to eat of the fruit of the tree of knowledge of good and evil, that same fruit which he had been forbidden to eat under the penalty of death.

In so doing, man lost his innocence and was driven from the paradise of pleasure. The earth was cursed in his disobedience. With much toil and labor now man must work to supply the most basic food and shelter for his survival.

Is Heaven, then, to be forever closed against him? Is the earth to be forever cursed in his work? Is there no one upon whom God can look contentedly, no one who has not been touched by the disease caused by Adam's disobedience?

There is one who escaped and whom God finds free from stain. The humble Virgin Mary, ever virgin, blessed among women. By a special preference of God, she was protected in her humility from the infection that came to all the children of Adam. She was the only one untouched by the withering wind of disobedience.

The archangel, prostrate before her in her humble home in Nazareth, salutes her, "Hail, full of grace, the Lord is with thee" (Luke 1:28). This is our Mother Mary, the fruit of whose chaste womb, Jesus, is to reopen Heaven, bring back blessings to earth and redemption and salvation to man.

Oh, spotless! Oh, ever blessed Virgin Mary! Oh, pure and immaculate Mother of our Redeemer, no stain is upon you. You are all fair in the sight of God. You are our sweet, our loving mother, untouched, even by original sin, from the first moment of your Immaculate Conception.

CHAPTER X
Mother Most Amiable

God loves His works and delights in them. His love is proportionate to the perfection of His handiwork. The greater the beauty that He finds in His creatures, the more amiable are they in His sight. But God has no work more exalted or perfect in His creation than Mary.

He might make a greater world, a more sublime Heaven, but not a nobler, better mother than His own most amiable Mother, Mary.

Her love for Him, arising from her fullness of grace, surpasses that of all the choirs of angels. Her heart is a very ocean of love. She loved and loves God more than all His other creatures united. In her is all beauty; in her are all virtues, all graces, all perfections that can be found in all the saints combined. She has united them in herself, as the ocean unites in itself the waters of all the rivers of the world.

In creating the universe, God but spoke the word. In creating Mary, "He hath showed might in His arm" (Luke 1:51).

An ardent love for God consumed her soul. She longed for the redemption of man, for the coming of the Messiah. It was all she thought and prayed about. Her prayer prevailed and God condescended to dwell in her womb and become man to save man.

How lovable, O Lord, is this, Thy tabernacle among men. Most dear to God the Father, Mary is no less amiable to her spouse, the Holy Spirit of God.

One of the great advocates and lovers of Mary, Saint Alphonsus de Liguori, tells us in his sermon on the Assumption of the Blessed Virgin that the Holy Ghost united Himself

The White Virgin, "La Virgen Blanca" was a gift from Saint Louis
IX of France to his cousin, Saint Ferdinand III of Castile. It can be
found in the Cathedral of Toledo, Spain.

to Mary as fire does to iron. He inflames her, consumes her,
and transforms her into His own love. He does this so com-
pletely that we see in her only the ardent flower of love of the
Holy Ghost.

She experiences only the fire of divine love. With reason is she called in Holy Scripture "the mother of fair love"
(Ecclus. 24:24).

If she is lovable to the Father and the Holy Spirit, how
much more amiable is she to God the Son, Whose mother
she is! Every son looks upon his mother as the most amiable

among women! He loves her tenderly, he sees in her only what is lovable. She is all and all to him, his life, his sweetness, his hope. She is to him the best, the greatest, the most beautiful of women. If such be the feeling of the ordinary son for his mother, what must be the devotion of Jesus for His most pure, amiable mother?

Being the only child born of her womb, He loves her wholly without having to share His affection with another. He belongs entirely to Mary. She has for Him an undivided love. Between them there is a perfect mutual love. They are to each other most amiable. Jesus knows and, in a Godlike manner, appreciates the lovable graces that adorn the soul and body of His mother. He is perfect and beautiful because all beauty and perfection are in Him; Mary is all beautiful for there is nothing defiled in her.

The integrity of her virginity makes her body lovable; the virtues of humility and chastity render her soul radiant with loveliness. Her body is as pure as the snow, her soul is spotless.

Mary is the Mother of Him Who is dignity itself. She is beautiful beside Eternal Beauty and immaculate in the presence of Him Who never knew sin. Great with the Most High, spouse of the Holy Ghost, Mary is the mother most amiable of Jesus. She conceived Him in her womb, nursed Him in His infancy and cared for Him throughout His childhood and young manhood. She accompanied Him in His journeys of kindness, love and charity.

In His sorrows she suffered with Him. She rejoiced with Him in His joys. She was always with Him, from the manger to the tomb. His Godlike devotion to her points out how amiable His Mother Mary was to Him.

CHAPTER XI
Mother Most Admirable

The heavens and the earth show forth the glory of God. All His works are wonderful. They magnify the name of the Lord. They sing His praises.

Yet, Saint Thomas Aquinas, the illustrious Doctor of the Church, declares that God could create nothing more glorious, nothing greater than the ever Blessed Virgin Mary, His most pure, most chaste, most admirable Mother.

We can see how true this is by observing the reverence and obedience Jesus had for her. That a creature should command her Creator, and that the Creator should obey His creature, is marvelous. One need only reflect on the wedding feast at Cana, Jesus' first miracle, to find proof of this.

She is so admirable that she possessed in her most chaste womb Him Whom the heavens and the earth could not contain.

God has received more honor, more glory from Mary than He has from all His other creatures in Heaven and on earth. She has honored Him in her greatness, born of her humility, in her devotion, in her graces and in the way that she profited by every gift or favor that she received from God.

The greatness of Mary far surpasses that of all of God's other creatures. Just as gold outvalues the basest metals, as Heaven is above the earth, as the light of the sun outshines that of all the other luminaries, so does Mary surpass all of creation. Before her greatness all other created greatness fades away as the light of the stars vanishes before the dazzling rays of the sun.

All the renowned women of the Old Testament—Sarah,

Deborah, Susanna, Judith, Esther and others—were but figures of Mary.

Of Judith it was said: "She was greatly renowned among all" (Jth. 8:8). In addressing her, Holofernes said: "Thou shalt be great [...] and thy name shall be renowned through all the earth" (Jth. 11:21). The people of Bethulia cried out to her as she passed: "Thou art the glory of Jerusalem; thou art the joy of Israel; thou art the honor of our people" (Jth. 15:10).

These titles are eminently applicable to Mary and are bestowed upon her by the Doctors and Fathers of the Church.

We owe all to God. In no way is He indebted to us. It is different with Mary. Though she has received all from Him, He became, so to speak, her debtor when Jesus Christ, His well-beloved Son, received His humanity from her flesh and blood.

In His conception and in His birth the God-man became indebted to her even more so than other children to their mother, for from her alone did He take the substance with which He would frame for Himself a human body.

Among all the children of men, from the dawn of creation and until the last of them shall be born into the world, there has not been nor can there be one as admirable as Mary. If you were to look among all the blessed spirits who are ministering angels at the throne of God, you would not find one more wonderful than the Blessed Virgin. Her sanctity, holiness, virtues, graces and perfections of body and soul are so great that she is more celebrated than all the saints and angels and thereby gives more glory and honor to God than all of them put together.

She is truly the unsurpassed Virgin Mary, to whom all the

saints and angels pay homage.

The Blessed Trinity honors her. She alone is the mother most pure, most chaste, most holy, most lovable. She alone is the Mother Most Admirable of the Second Person of the Godhead, Christ Jesus, the Redeemer and Savior of the world.

CHAPTER XII
Mother of Good Counsel

"He that is mighty, has done great things to me" (Luke 1:49). We shall know only in the Kingdom of God the wonderful things He did for the Mother of His Divine Son.

From all eternity, Mary was prominently before the mind of God. In her, "He hath showed might in His arm" (Luke 1:51). She is the masterpiece of His creation. He endowed her mind, heart and soul with all graces. He hailed her through one of His ministering spirits, "full of grace" (Luke 1:28).

Is it any wonder, then, that Holy Mother Church uses many endearing titles to invoke her aid in the Litany recited in her honor? All the invocations used in this form of prayer are fitting tributes of respect to her.

For example, in a vision she appeared to Saint Dominic and counseled him that in order to overcome the heresy of the Albigenses he should preach the devotion of the rosary. Hence we invoke her as "Queen of the Holy Rosary."

More recently, she appeared to a simple and humble child of the people and gave to Saint Bernadette as her name, the one by which she desired to be known and honored: "I am the Immaculate Conception," Queen conceived without sin, our Queen Immaculate.

More than five hundred years have come and gone since the day when, midst the chanting of angels and the spontaneous pealing of bells, a picture, known as the "Mother of Good Counsel," made its appearance in Genazzano, Italy. The image is there to this day, where it is still being venerated by tens of thousands of pilgrims every year. This miraculous

Shrine of the miraculous fresco of the Mother of Good Counsel of Genazzano, Italy.

picture, the source of numerous miracles, was first honored in a small sanctuary dedicated to the Annunciation of the Blessed Virgin at Scutari in Albania.

How this beautiful image of Mary Most Holy holding the infant Christ in her arms traveled from Albania to Italy is a marvel all its own. Misfortune visited the sanctuary where she first resided, because most of the people who lived there failed to recognize and profit by the many favors Heaven bestowed upon them. Pride and the delirium of pleasure wrecked Albania's reason. It persecuted the children of God, rejected His Holy Word, and after many unrighteous conflicts, fell from the unity of the Faith.

Weary of its evil ways, God visited Albania with a scourge terrible in its consequences. As Attila in his day proved to be the scourge of God, so now the Turks were the means in His Hands to chastise the wayward Albanians.

With the help of divine grace, some of the inhabitants preserved their piety and held steadfastly to the Catholic Faith. Some of these resolved to leave a land where they were not free to worship their God as they felt it their duty to do. They resolved to seek a place where they would not be molested in their religious obligations.

Of those who had determined to leave Albania, there were two devoted clients of Mary, Mother of Good Counsel, Giorgio and De Sclavis. It was the practice of these two devoted servants of the Blessed Virgin to kneel in prayer before the picture of Our Lady of Good Counsel. They would ask her to obtain a blessing upon unfortunate Albania and to direct them in their undertakings.

Mary advised them to seek a home elsewhere, and that she herself in the image which they revered, would also depart from a land so hostile to her and her Divine Son. Genazzano of Latium, in Italy, was the place chosen by Our Lady of Good Counsel where she would henceforth be honored.

And then the unbelievable occurred. It was on the twenty-fifth of April, 1467, that the miraculous picture, descending from a radiant cloud, rested on an unfinished wall of the Church of Saint Biagio.

Many residents of that part of Italy were gathered there on that day and saw the image of Our Lady of Good Counsel descending upon their church. As you can imagine, they were overcome with awe and admiration. Since then Genazzano has been the mecca of armies of pilgrims from Italy and other countries, who seek temporal and spiritual favors through Mary, the Mother of Good Counsel.

She is the seat of wisdom, which she possessed from the beginning. Through her inspirations we are able to turn aside from evil ways, into the only secure way of life. She admonishes us, by both word and example, to seek above all things the Kingdom of Heaven. She is its gate, and to enter it we must heed her wise counsels, and follow her life as closely as it is in our power to do.

Our vocation is to be saints. To reach the goal, Mary, Star of the Sea, will guide us over the troubled waters of life, if we allow the light of her wisdom to enter our souls.

The will of God is our sanctification. We cannot fail to attain sanctity if we follow the inspiration of Mary's counsels, humbly accepting the dispensations of His divine providence towards us.

In joy and in sorrow; in poverty and in riches; in happiness and in afflictions; in sickness and in health, let us seek the advice of our sweet, loving Mother of Good Counsel, that we may possess with her the virtue to keep our soul in peace, and to bless the name of God even in times of great distress.

She will be our life, our sweetness, our hope; and the beneficial influence of her wisdom will prove her to be our Mother of Good Counsel.

CHAPTER XIII
Mother of Our Creator

Mysteries surround us. We live, move, and have our being, so to speak, in the midst of mysteries. There are marvels in the heavens, on the earth, in the waters, under the waters and in ourselves.

We know so little of the secrets of God. We have such an imperfect understanding of the ways of Divine Providence. We cannot fathom God's infinite wisdom. His designs are mysterious. We cannot know the mind of God. Our finite mind is powerless to comprehend the works of the Almighty Being.

As the child accepts without questioning the word of his father, so must we, even more so, receive the word of God as our way, our light and our life.

One of the most profound mysteries we are asked to believe in is that of the Most Blessed Trinity. One God, yet three Divine Persons. It is a dogma of Catholic faith. It is a teaching of Holy Scripture, a divinely revealed truth.

The Father is God, the Son is God, the Holy Ghost is God, nevertheless there is but one God. The Father is from all eternity, the Son had no beginning and will have no end, and the Holy Ghost is the Alpha and Omega of all things. But they are not three eternals, they are but one eternal God, Who is the Creator of the heavens and the earth.

God the Father alone is not the Creator, neither is the Son, nor is the Holy Ghost, but the Father, Son and Holy Ghost, the triune God, is the Creator of all things.

God the Son, the Second Person of the Adorable Trinity, became man in assuming our human nature. Still, He did not cease to be God, for as God He is eternal, in whom there can be neither change nor alteration.

Mary is the woman of God's special predilection. When, in the fullness of time, according to the designs of the Almighty, the Second Person of the Godhead was to become man, it was in her chaste womb that the Second Person of the Holy Trinity was to nestle and take to Himself her flesh and blood, and become man. She is, therefore, His Mother, the Mother of the God-man Who was born of her.

"Behold a virgin shall be with child, and bring forth a son, and they shall call His name Emmanuel, which being interpreted is, God with us" (Matt. 1:23). And the Angel said to Mary: "Behold thou shalt conceive in thy womb, and shalt bring forth a Son; and thou shalt call His name Jesus. He shall be great, and shall be called the Son of the Most High" (Luke 1:31, 32). This Emmanuel, this Son of the Most High, is none other than the Son of the ever glorious Virgin Mary. Her Son is the Second Person of the Most Blessed Trinity, true God equal to His Father. He is our Creator. But Mary, being His Mother, is the Mother of our Creator.

Marvel of marvels, that a creature should become the Mother of her Creator! But what a creature she is, who surpasses in dignity, in virtue and in grace all the angels and saints of God. Virgin of Virgins, spotless, most pure Mary, chosen from all eternity to be the glorious and immaculate Mother of our Creator.

CHAPTER XIV
Mother of Our Redeemer

God created man in a state of innocence, and made him to His own image and likeness. He fitted for him a beautiful home, a paradise on earth. Eden was to be his home for a short time only, after which he would be taken up to his true home, the celestial paradise.

In order for man's happiness to continue during his earthly pilgrimage and be his inheritance for all eternity in the mansions of Heaven, he must remain faithful to the state of innocence in which he was created. To lose his innocence was to forfeit his happiness both for time and eternity.

As we are all painfully aware, that first man trespassed against the command of his Creator, by eating that which he had been forbidden to eat, namely, the fruit of the tree of the knowledge of good and evil. Instantly he was driven out of the Garden of Eden, and in his disobedience lost also his right to the Kingdom of Heaven.

Yet, God did not leave man without hope. Before punishing him, he gave to him the promise of a Redeemer. This Redeemer would rescue him from the dreadful ruin he had brought upon himself and his descendants.

Man's transgression was infinite in its consequences, as it was an offense against the infinite majesty of an Almighty Being. Only an action of infinite proportion could repair the damage done and make atonement for the outrage that had occurred. Who could be found whose merits would suffice to make this fitting and requisite atonement?

Could it be a child of Adam? No, all men are born with the stain of their first parent's sin on their souls. Perhaps it could be one of the bright spirits ministering at the throne of the Creator? No, they are created, and are therefore finite. In their nature, they are incapable of infinite merit.

God alone can accomplish the work of man's redemption, for He alone is infinite. But will He condescend to repair a wrong done against His divine majesty? He will, for He gave His promise to our first parents that He would send them a Redeemer. He is the God of mercy and of charity. He is our God, our Father, Who loves us, sinful though we be, with an infinite love.

"By this," declares Saint John, "has the charity of God appeared toward us, because God has sent His only begotten Son into the world, that we may live by Him" (1 John 4:9). "For God so loved the world," says the Holy Scriptures, "as to give His only begotten Son" (John 3:16).

By these words of the Holy Scriptures we readily discern the burning love our Heavenly Father has for us. Now, listen to the declaration of love for us by the Son of God in addressing His Father: "Sacrifice and oblation thou wouldst not [have]; but a body thou hast fitted to me. Holocausts for sin did not please thee. Then said I: 'Behold I come; that I should do Thy will, O God'" (Heb. 10:5-7).

Our Divine Lord offered Himself to God for our redemption and He will come and save us. Hence, Saint Paul, writing to Timothy, says: "Christ Jesus came into this world to save sinners, of whom I am the chief" (1 Tim. 1:15). And again: "For there is one God, and one mediator of God and men, the man Christ Jesus: Who gave Himself in redemption for all" (1 Tim. 2:5-6). To Titus the same Apostle asserts that, Christ Jesus "gave Himself for us, that He might redeem us from all iniquity, and might cleanse to Himself a people acceptable, a pursuer of good works" (Titus 2:14). "The blood of Jesus

Lamentation over the Dead Christ (1436-1441) by Fra Angelico, tempera on wood, detail.

Christ," asserts Saint John, "cleanses us from all sin" (1 John 1:7). "And He is the propitiation for our sins; and not for ours only, but also for those of the whole world" (1 John 2:2). "For this is good," writes Saint Paul to Timothy, "and acceptable in the sight of God our Savior, who will have all men to be saved, and to come to the knowledge of the truth" (1 Tim. 2:3-4).

For this reason the same Apostle assures us that, "Christ died for all; that they also who live, may not now live to themselves, but unto Him who died for them, and rose again" (2 Cor. 5:15). In this way did our Lord effect our reconciliation with God. In the shedding of His blood is our victory over the devil, the world and the flesh.

"Thou art worthy," sang the angels in a new canticle, "O Lord, to take the book, and to open the seals thereof; because Thou was slain and have redeemed us to God, in Thy blood, out of every tribe, and tongue, and people, and nation. And hast made us to our God a kingdom and priests, and we shall reign" (Apoc. 5:9-10).

But how did our Savior come to live among us? What means did God choose to send into the world the Redeemer He promised to man? It was through the indescribable mystery of the Incarnation. Herein the Son of God became man. Having promised from the beginning of time to take unto Himself our human nature and become our Redeemer by suffering in the flesh and dying on the Cross for us, He descended from Heaven, took up His abode in the most pure womb of the humble Virgin of Nazareth, and was born of her.

Equal to His Father and yet a man, the only Son of the Blessed Virgin Mary was able, through His bloody passion and death as man, to raise the merits of His clean oblation to an infinite value by His union with the Godhead. In this way He was able to satisfy the infinite justice of His Father, and accomplish the redemption of the world.

But Mary, most loving, most pure, Mary immaculate, is the Mother of the Son of God, the Second Person of the Blessed Trinity, the Redeemer of men.

CHAPTER XV
Virgin Most Prudent

Saint Thomas teaches that prudence is the eye of the soul, the pilot of all its movements and actions. Therefore, it is no wonder that the great Apostle warns us of its necessity. "See, therefore, brethren, how you walk circumspectly: not as unwise, but as wise: redeeming the time, because the days are evil. Wherefore, become not unwise, but understanding what is the will of God. And [...] be ye filled with the Holy Spirit" (Eph. 5:15-18).

"My Son," says the Lord in the Book of Proverbs, "attend to My wisdom and incline thy ear to My prudence. That thou mayest keep thoughts and thy lips may preserve instruction" (Prov. 5:1, 2). If we practice the virtue of prudence, we will keep a watch upon our thoughts, so that nothing will take root in our minds but that which is godly. We will watch what we say, so that our speech will always be holy and charitable. We will govern our actions so as to render them pleasing and acceptable in the sight of God.

When our Savior sent His apostles to teach the maxims of the Gospel to men and nations, He bade them to be prudent: "Behold, I send you as sheep in the midst of wolves. Be therefore wise as serpents" (Matt. 10:16). They are cautioned that while they are commissioned to carry the Gospel to all peoples, they must watch and pray and be prudent, so as not to be deceived by their artful ways. Even though they must be in the world, they must not be of it.

Prudence urges us to keep the law of God and to meditate upon it. We must know the rewards that follow its observance, and the punishments that are meted out to those who transgress it, so that we may walk justly and piously before God. Prudence purifies the soul, regulates the heart, overcomes excesses and gives us knowledge of things human and divine. It brightens our pathway through the world. It steers our fragile boat of this life safely and serenely over breakers and hidden shoals.

"If thou shalt incline thy ear to prudence," says the Book of Proverbs, "If thou shalt seek her as money, and shalt dig for her as for a treasure, then shalt thou understand the fear of the Lord, and shalt find the knowledge of God. Because the Lord giveth wisdom, and out of His mouth cometh prudence and knowledge" (Prov. 2:3-6). Prudence teaches and predisposes us to know, to love and to serve God with all our mind, with all our strength, with all our soul. It helps us to shun evil and to do that which is good. It is the knowledge of the saints.

Among the beautiful parables whereby our Savior illustrated His teachings, there is one especially on prudence spoken privately to His apostles, that of the ten virgins. They were invited to a marriage feast and set out with their lamps to meet the bridal party. Five of them failed to carry with them any extra supply of oil, in case of an emergency. Practicing prudence, the other five had a quantity of it in their vessels, besides what was in their lamps.

When they reached the appointed place where they were to meet the bride and groom, there was a delay, as the bridal party had not arrived. While waiting, the ten virgins slumbered. Towards midnight they were awakened and told to be in readiness for the bridegroom was approaching. Quickly they arose and set about trimming their lamps. Five of them discovered that while they slept the oil in their lamps became exhausted. They called upon the other virgins, who had some in their vessels, to divide it with them. But those refused, lest they, too, might not have sufficient to last them. The prudent virgins advised those who ran short of oil to run to the venders and purchase what they might need.

During their absence the bridegroom came and was met by the five whose lamps were burning, and they proceeded to the marriage feast. When those, who had to seek more oil, returned they found the door shut against them. They pleaded with the bridegroom to allow them to enter, but he answering, said, "I know you not."

The five virgins who brought oil in their vessels are called the five wise or prudent virgins, while the other five are known as the five unwise or foolish virgins.

Mary, the Virgin of Virgins, carried always with her, not only the oil that kept her lamp burning, but also a vessel overflowing with it. From this vessel, she could even supply others who would call upon her for it. For she is the Virgin, "full of grace," full of the oil of divine love.

Prudence characterized all her words and works. Prudence was the jewel of her whole life. She loved and cultivated it day by day. She was never found without the oil of sanctity. Her prudence was a buckler that shielded her against the loss of her sublime virtues that made her so admirable in the sight of God. Hence, we hail her as the most wise, most prudent Virgin Mary.

CHAPTER XVI
Virgin Most Venerable

W e read in the Book of Wisdom that, "venerable old age is not that of long time, nor counted by the number of years: but [...] a spotless life is old age" (Wisd. 4:8, 9).

From these words of Holy Scripture we are given to understand that it is not gray hair, whitened by the snows of many winters, that make us venerable, but rather the purity of our life.

We are not to determine one's worth by the number of years one has lived, but how he has lived during those years. A venerable life is conspicuous for its merits. It is a spotless life; a life that goes on not for a few days or years, but for ages. When our lives are irreproachable, they are venerable, whether they be of short or long duration.

The patriarchs were venerable, not so much for the length of their years as for their upright lives. The prophets, apostles, martyrs, virgins, in a word, all the saints attained a venerable age, whatever the number of their days, because of their holy lives. They live in the memory of men and will live through the endless ages in eternal glory.

If a spotless life is indeed venerable, how supremely venerable must be that of the Virgin of Virgins, Mary, ever Virgin, whose purity of body and soul transcends that of all the saints and angels more than the light of the sun surpasses that of all the stars in the firmament.

How incomprehensible is the difference between the small drop of rain that falls to earth from the clouds and the immense body of water of the ocean! How incalculably insignificant is the grain of sand upon the seashore if you would compare it to the innumerable grains of sand that form all the beaches of all the oceans of the world!

And yet, immensely greater than these is the chasm that exists between all the holy virgins of God and the immaculate Virgin Mary, Mother of Christ, our Redeemer.

If a spotless life is venerable, is not Mary the immaculate most venerable? At her birth the very angels cry out: "Who is she that comes forth as the morning rising, fair as the moon, bright as the sun, terrible as an army set in array?" (Cant. 6:9).

She is the daughter of the Eternal Father, the spouse of the Holy Ghost, the Virgin Mother of Jesus, and there is not a spot in her.

CHAPTER XVII
Virgin Most Renowned

In Heaven the virgins are especially privileged and hold a renowned place. "They sing as it were a new canticle before the throne; for they are virgins. These follow the Lamb wherever He goes. For they are without spot before the throne of God" (Apoc. 14: 3-5).

Virgins are more renowned than the angels. For when God promised them the highest place and the greatest name, he manifested His predilection for them over the angels. Virginity in the angels is not by virtue, they are by nature virgins, whereas those who, by choice and heroic virtue, select to live the life of a virgin are more venerable, more exalted before God.

The superiority of Mary's virginity is readily understood, since she of all virgins was chosen by the Creator on account of her loftier virginity, to be the Mother of the Word made flesh. The fullness of the divinity dwelt physically in her. She was found "full of grace," worthy to conceive the Savior, to bring into the world the Life of the world and remain always a virgin, to be the Virgin Most Renowned.

Of herself she spoke the prophetic words: "All generations shall call me blessed" (Luke 1:48). Blessed because of her virginity and divine motherhood. The prophecy has had its fulfillment in all past generations, as it will have in all future generations, and for all eternity.

The churches, chapels, shrines and altars erected in her honor; the praises bestowed upon her; the pilgrimages made to invoke her aid or thank her for favors received; the prayers that are daily offered to her by the faithful everywhere, are so many testimonials of her prophetic words: "All generations shall call me blessed."

Not only among men has our most loving Mother Mary obtained renown, but she is celebrated among all the angels in Heaven. She repaired the losses they sustained by the expulsion from Heaven of the fallen angels. She changed the gloom and sorrow that rested upon man into hope and cheer; she broke the chains of slavery that manacled woman; she brought joy to those who died in the Lord by ending their captivity.

Her name is invoked by and honored among angels and men. The angels salute her as "full of grace." Men sing her praises because she is the Mother of their Savior, Jesus. All call her blessed, who is Virgin of Virgins and Mother Immaculate. She is the most renowned of all of God's creatures.

CHAPTER XVIII
Virgin Most Powerful

The ever glorious and blessed Virgin Mary was prefigured in the Old Testament by many great and distinguished women. Among them we find the peerless heroine, Judith, who was especially renowned by her bravery and strength.

Her people, the people of Israel, were in imminent danger of falling into the hands of Holofernes, who was enslaving all around him, obliging the conquered to bow down before the king Nebuchadnezzar and worship him as their god. In his conquests he approached a town, Bethulia, occupied by the Israelites, and sent his army to besiege the city. Dread took hold upon the people. They feared falling into the hands of Holofernes, which meant that they should either worship the king or be put to a most cruel death.

There lived among them a very holy servant of God, Judith. Filled with the spirit of God, she addressed the ancients of the people, she encouraged them to pray and to rely on the power of the God of Israel. They asked her to beseech the Lord for them, as she was a holy woman. Judith took leave of them, retired to pray and prepared herself for her undertaking. She besought the God of Hosts to grant her loyalty in mind and fortitude in her purpose of overthrowing Holofernes. "For," she exclaimed, "this will be a glorious monument for Thy name, when he shall fall by the hand of a woman" (Jth. 9:15).

She went forth into the camp of the Assyrians, was apprehended by them and taken to Holofernes. This is what she wanted to happen. Having ingratiated herself into the good will of the general, she accomplished her design. By the grace

"Who is she that cometh forth as the morning rising, fair as the moon, bright as the sun, terrible as an army set in array." (Cant. 6:9). Statue of Our Lady of the Rosary of Lepanto, Granada, Spain.

of God, she had the courage to decapitate him, and straightway returned to her people.

"Praise ye the Lord our God," she said to them, for "by me, His handmaid, He has fulfilled His mercy, which He promised to the house of Israel; and He has killed the enemy of

His people by my hand this night. [...] Behold the head of Holofernes, the general of the army of the Assyrians, the Lord our God slew him by the hand of a woman" (Jth. 13:17-19).

The achievement of Judith foreshadowed the power to be displayed by the most powerful of the servants of God, Mary, ever Virgin, in the part taken by her in our Redemption.

The time had come for God to fulfill the promise made to man in the garden of Paradise, to send him a Redeemer who would deliver him from the slavery of the most wicked one. For this he chose His handmaid, the spotless Virgin Mary. Through her He struck the wily serpent, and beneath her heel crushed his head. "But the Almighty Lord," said Judith, "has struck him and has delivered him into the hands of a woman, and has slain him" (Jth. 6:7).

She, the humble Virgin of Nazareth, by her perfect purity, found favor in the sight of the Almighty God. He looked complacently upon the beauty and humility of His handmaid and gave her power over the enemy of His people, that she might overthrow him and free those in bondage.

Of her is born the Savior, Who put Satan to flight, conquered the powers of darkness, and reopened heaven. Where sin abounded, grace still more abounds. All was lost, now all is redeemed.

Not only one people is saved, but all men and nations are set free through Jesus, the Son of the Virgin of Virgins, Virgin most pure and most chaste. She is the Mother of Jesus, the Redeemer of all men. She is the Queen of all the angels, the power of God's strong arm.

On earth and in Heaven, by men and by angels, she is hailed as the Virgin most powerful, since all have enjoyed the fruits of the power that He who is almighty gave to her.

CHAPTER XIX
Virgin Most Merciful

Out of pure mercy, Jesus spoke the word to His eternal Father: "Behold, I come." Out of pure mercy, Mary spoke the word to the Almighty: "Behold, the Handmaid of the Lord." By the word of Jesus the Redemption of men was made possible; by the word of Mary, the way was at hand through which the Savior could come into the world.

The Apostle Saint Paul calls God, "the Father of mercies, and the God of all comfort" (2 Cor. 1:3). Mary may well be styled the mother of all mercies and the queen of all comfort. Her feelings of tender love for poor fallen humanity are as wings upon which she comes to the help of those who invoke her aid.

Saint Anselm assures us that salvation at times is more certain through the invocation of Mary, the most merciful Virgin, than by appealing to Jesus Himself. Jesus, as our judge, must inflict punishment, whereas Mary, our sweet, loving Mother, has only a feeling of mercy for us.

Saint Bernard has well said: "Let Him, O Blessed Virgin, deny your mercy who shall have called upon you in vain in the hour of distress! Who, O Blessed Virgin, can sound the width, the height and the depth of your mercy?" (Serm. IV de Assump. B.M.V.).

It was through the compassionate mercy of Mary that Jesus performed His first miracle at the marriage of Cana, when He changed water into wine. Her mercy for us caused her to follow in the footsteps of her Divine Son, as He bore upon His bruised and bleeding shoulders the heavy weight of the cross, laden, as it was, with our sins.

Out of pure mercy for suffering humanity, Mary stood beneath the cross of her Son, Jesus, and made the offering of her heart's blood in that of the Sacred Heart of Jesus for our redemption. Did not her most loving soul repeat the words of mercy spoken by our Lord upon the Cross: "Father, forgive them, for they know not what they do?" (Luke 23:34). She knew His innocence. She understood His generous heart. She was well aware that He was giving His life for those who persecuted Him and nailed Him to the Cross. No word of complaint or reproach escaped her lips, but with a heart full of mercy and a soul full of compassion, she pleaded with an outraged God for mercy upon the heads of an ungrateful people.

When the lifeless body of her Jesus was lowered from the cross and laid in her arms, she pressed her dead Son to her loving bosom, as she did so often in His lifetime, during His infancy and childhood. Even in that trying moment she prayed that His mercy might go out to all the generations of men. His infinite love for them would bring them to the throne of mercy, that with her they might bless for all eternity, Him whom they so unmercifully put to death.

While Jesus rose triumphant from the dead and ascended into Heaven to plead there with His Father for mercy for all men, Mary remained on earth to be among men a merciful mother asking Heaven for mercy.

With contrite and loving hearts we should constantly turn to her now that she is enthroned in glory beside her Divine Son, and say to her: "O Mother of Clemency, our life, our sweetness and our hope, turn your eyes of mercy towards us, and after this, our exile, show to us the fruit of your womb, our merciful Redeemer, Jesus."

CHAPTER XX
Virgin Most Faithful

"My meat," said Jesus to His Disciples, "is to do the will of Him who sent me." (John 4:34). The faithful performance of the mission which He had received from His heavenly Father was the consuming object of the life of our Lord on earth.

While praying in the garden of Olives, our Lord underwent a dreadful agony. The storm of sorrows loomed up before Him, and He prayed to His heavenly Father: "My Father, if it be possible, let this chalice pass from Me. Nevertheless not as I will, but as Thou wilt" (Matt. 26:39).

"He humbled Himself, becoming obedient unto death, even to the death of the Cross" (Phil. 2:8). In the beautiful prayer He has taught us, He tells us to say: "Thy will, [O my Father], be done on earth as it is in Heaven" (Matt. 6:10).

He was faithful to His word, given from all eternity, "behold, I come," when He came down from Heaven, assumed our human nature and dwelt among us. As a child He was obedient and faithful to His Mother and His foster-father, Saint Joseph, for "He went down with them and came to Nazareth and was subject to them" (Luke 2:51).

He was faithful in the home of His Mother and in the workshop of Saint Joseph. He was faithful in the work of His Father among the Jews. He was even faithful to His will before the judge who condemned Him to death, before the uncouth soldiers who struck Him in the face, spat upon Him, scourged Him, crowned Him with thorns, placed the heavy load of the Cross upon Him and nailed Him to it, whereon He hung until He died.

"Maria Santissima de la Candelaria" in the Church of St. Nicholas of Bari, Seville, Spain.

Who among the servants of God, who among the followers of Christ will most closely follow the faithfulness of Jesus to the will of His Father? Shall it be one of the patriarchs or prophets; one of the apostles or martyrs; one of the confessors or saints? Or shall it be one of the ministering angels at the throne of God? The former had but few opportunities under the humbling hand of God, wherein to prove their fidelity to His word; the latter had but one to test theirs.

Is there no one to follow the faithful Jesus from the cradle to the grave? God be praised, there was one, the Virgin most faithful, His own Virgin Mother Mary. From the first instant of her Immaculate Conception, she was full of grace. In her childhood she consecrated herself to God, to do His will in all things.

In the middle of great confusion of mind and soul, she exclaimed: "Behold the handmaid of the Lord, be it done to me according to Thy word" (Luke 1:38). She kept the secret of God in her heart until He Himself chose to reveal it to her chaste spouse, Saint Joseph. "Joseph, son of David, fear not to take unto thee Mary, thy wife, for that which is conceived in her, is of the Holy Ghost" (Matt. 1:20).

Through His childhood, youth and young manhood, she continued still faithful to God's design upon the Child, and did not reveal it until Jesus Himself chose to do so. She was faithful to Him during the last three years of His life, when He went about doing the work of His Father.

Is it any wonder, then, that He should have praised her for her fidelity to God's word, rather than for being His Mother? On one occasion while He preached, a woman cried out, "Blessed is the womb that bore thee, and the breast that gave Thee suck." Our Lord responded, "Yea, rather, blessed are they who hear the word of God and keep it" (Luke 11:27-28). Mary treasured every word of His and continuously pondered them in her heart.

With Christ, her Divine Son, she was faithful to God, even during the tragedy of the cross. She would have died beneath it for love of Him. But God sustained her in order that she might be faithful to the end in her mission among men. Her whole life was one act of entire submission to His holy will.

She had no thought except to please Him. She spoke no word but to magnify His name. She performed no work unless it was a work of mercy. She was faithful to her Immaculate Conception and to the many graces bestowed upon her. She was faithful to the will of the Father, true to the love of her Spouse, the Holy Ghost, and constant in her devotion to her Divine Son.

CHAPTER XXI
Mirror of Justice

God, Who is infinite perfection, is infinite justice. Every conceivable or possible perfection is in Him in an infinite degree so that the union of them all constitute in Him but one infinite perfection, since He is the only infinite Being. There is nothing, nor can there be anything, wanting in Him.

"Glorify the Lord as much as ever you can, for He will yet far exceed, and His magnificence is wonderful. Blessing the Lord, exalt Him as much as you can, for He is above all praise. When you exalt Him, put forth all your strength, and be not weary: for you can never go far enough. Who shall see Him, and declare Him? And who shall magnify Him as He is from the beginning" (Ecclus. 43:32-35). The more you study, admire, praise and magnify Him, the more scope you find to study, admire, praise and glorify Him.

In comparison to what He is, all our admiration, all our hymns of praise to Him are less than the grain of sand compared to the universe, less than the dew drop, compared with the oceans of the world. Infinite in all things, there is nothing that can be added to Him. He gives of His treasures without lessening or change in Him. Whatever of perfection there is in the angels, in men, in all His creatures, it is in Him without limit, infinitely. He is infinite justice, because He is infinite perfection.

Infinite wisdom, says the Holy Scripture, "reaches from end to end mightily and orders all things sweetly" (Wisd. 8:1).

In the incarnation, God, according to His infinite justice, brought together two extremes: the infinite and the finite, the divine and the human. All was in disorder, but in becoming

Miraculous statue of Our Lady of Good Success in the Conceptionist Convent of the Immaculate Conception in Quito, Ecuador.

man, God reestablished harmony everywhere and in all things.

"Behold," says the Prophet Isaiah, "a virgin shall conceive and bear a Son, and His name shall be called Emmanuel" (Isa. 7:14). Saint Paul tells us Who He is: "And evidently great is the mystery of godliness, which was manifested in the flesh, was justified in the spirit, appeared unto angels, has been preached unto the Gentiles, is believed in the world, is taken up in glory" (1 Tim. 3:16).

He is the Word made flesh, true God and true man. As God, He is equal in all things to His Father. He possesses infinite justice, which is infinite perfection. The Incarnation is the masterpiece of the Almighty, more stupendous than the creation of the universe.

There is an infinitely wider difference between God and man than there is between the world and nothingness. Man, the king of creation, is finite, so that the difference between him and nothingness is not infinite, while it is infinite between God and His creature.

But Mary, the ever glorious Virgin Mother of God, is the masterpiece of His creation. She possesses, to a superior degree, all graces and all perfections. There is neither spot nor stain in her. Of all creatures, she is the nearest and dearest to God. She is the marvel of creation, the prodigy of the universe.

God's creation speaks to us of Him: the grain of sand, the snowflake, the drop of rain, the insect, and those things that are not visible to the naked eye. The sun in the heavens reflects His brightness, the moon His beauty, the ocean His immensity, the universe His greatness. If all nature mirrors His perfection, how much more beautifully is He reflected in the masterpiece of His creation, Mary? In God are all perfections. In Mary are all perfections. In God they are infinite, in Mary, they are necessarily finite.

Justice is the union of all perfections. Therefore, God is infinite justice. Mary is but finite justice, yet in a degree above that of all other creatures. She mirrors, therefore, more perfectly God's infinite justice than do all the kingdoms of creation. Truly, then, is she the Mirror of Justice.

CHAPTER XXII
Seat of Wisdom

Saint Paul gives us an insight into the wisdom and knowledge of God in his Epistle to the Romans.

"O the depth of the riches of the wisdom and of the knowledge of God! How incomprehensible are His judgments, and how unsearchable His ways! For who has known the mind of the Lord? Or who has been His counsellor? For of Him, and by Him, and in Him, are all things" (Rom. 11:33-34, 36).

Wisdom is the very essence of God. He is eternal wisdom, and from Him must all wisdom come. Wisdom "is an infinite treasure to men; which they that use, become the friends of God. For in her is the spirit of understanding: holy, one, manifold, subtle, eloquent, active, undefiled, sure, sweet, loving that which is good, quick, which nothing hinders, beneficent, gentle, kind, steadfast, assured, secure, having all power, overseeing all things, and containing all spirits, intelligible, pure.

"She is a vapor of the power of God, and a certain pure emanation of the glory of the Almighty God: and, therefore, no defiled thing will come into her.

"For she is the brightness of eternal light, and the unspotted mirror of God's majesty, and the image of His goodness. For God loves none but him that dwells with wisdom" (Wisd. 7:14, 22-26, 28). From this eloquent description of wisdom, we find out that God loves only those who dwell with wisdom.

But what do we learn about wisdom in the New Testament? Saint Paul writes of Jesus Christ, the well-beloved Son of Eternal Wisdom, "In whom are hid all the treasures of wisdom and knowledge" (Col. 2:3).

"But we preach Christ crucified, unto the Jews, indeed,

a stumbling block, and unto the Gentiles foolishness: but unto them that are called, both Jews and Greeks, Christ the power of God, and the wisdom of God" (1 Cor. 1:23-24).

The Apostle declares that true wisdom is to know Christ

and Him crucified, for the knowledge of Christ and His cross *is* wisdom. "We speak of wisdom, but not the wisdom of this world, neither of the princes of this world that come to naught; but we speak the wisdom of God in a mystery, a wisdom which is hidden, which God ordained before the world, unto our glory: which none of the princes of this world knew; for if they had known it, they would never have crucified the Lord of glory." (1 Cor. 2:6-8).

It is, therefore, wisdom to know Jesus Christ and what He has endured for us. It is to have a knowledge of Christ and of His cross, of His grace, of the Incarnation, of redemption, salvation and eternal glory. All these heavenly blessings come to us through Jesus who is the wisdom of His Father. True wisdom consists in knowing, loving and serving God above

Statue depicting Our Lady Seat of Wisdom.

all things; it helps us to follow Jesus and to praise and thank Him with our whole heart and soul.

Mary loves, above all men and angels, God and Jesus best.

God said to Solomon: "Ask what thou wilt that I should have to give it to thee." Solomon answered, "Give me wisdom and knowledge."

"And God said to Solomon: Because this choice hath pleased your heart, and you have not asked for riches, and wealth, and glory, nor the lives of them that hate thee, nor many days of life: but have asked for wisdom and knowledge; [...] wisdom and knowledge are granted to thee" (2 Chron. 1:7, 10, 11-12). Solomon received the gift of wisdom that he might serve God wisely and rule his people, over whom God had placed him, with justice.

Mary is called to govern, not one people, but all men and nations through the blessed fruit of her womb, Jesus, the Redeemer and Savior of the world. To rule wisely and in entire conformity to the will of her Creator, she asks Him that she should remain always a virgin most pure. So acceptable was this to God that He assured her that she should remain immaculate and that a more intimate union should exist between them. He would, in the person of His Divine Son, dwell in her most chaste womb and be born of her.

Eternal Wisdom would take up His abode in her, and our Mother Mary, our sweet loving Mother, would be the throne, the Seat of Wisdom among men.

CHAPTER XXIII
Cause of Our Joy

Jesus Christ is the real, the infinite source of our joy. Unfortunately for the human race, sin entered into the heart of the first man and drew upon him and his descendants misery and death.

The pleasant relationship between the Creator and His creatures was severed; their close union was broken. God sought man, after his fall, where He was wont to meet and talk with him. But man fled from the face of his Creator, knowing that he was no longer worthy to appear before Him.

It was a sad situation for man. Was it to be like this forever? Was no reconciliation to be brought about; had peace fled from his soul for all time?

No, the merciful Savior made reparation for the wrong and restored man to the friendship of his Creator. Jesus, our loving Lord, is our joy, for we were slaves and He freed us. He loved us even unto death, the humiliating death of the cross.

Our joy is found in the mercy of God, Who will heed the prayer and accept the sacrifice of His well-beloved Son for us. "Let your soul rejoice in His mercy" (Ecclus. 51:37). It rests on our confidence and hope in God. "For my hope is in the Eternal, and joy is come upon me from the Holy One" (Bar. 4:22).

It comes from God's own promise to us. He promised Adam to send a Savior who would crush the head of the devil and restore peace to the heart of man. The Lord of Hosts said, "I Myself will comfort you" (Isa. 51:12). "Then shall the virgin rejoice in the dance, the young men and the old men together: and I will turn their mourning into joy, and will comfort them, and make them joyful after their sorrow. And I will fill the soul of the priests with fatness: and my people shall be filled with My good things, said the Lord" (Jer. 31:13-14).

The coming of our Redeemer in our midst and the merits of His passion and death applied to us, all give joyfulness to our souls. In his day the prophet Habakkuk exclaimed: "I will rejoice in the Lord: and I will joy in God my Jesus" (Hab. 3:18).

Hundreds of years before the coming of the Redeemer, the prophet announced His name and rejoiced in Him. He foresaw that through Jesus all would be delivered from the slavery of the wicked one, and that we would be blessed and would rejoice in Him. Happy is the soul that responds to the love of Jesus. He is our joy, our peace, our life. He is our all.

But who is the woman promised by the Almighty, whose seed should be our Savior Jesus, the joy of the human race? All generations know her and call her blessed.

She is none other than the humble Virgin Mary of Nazareth, the Mother of Jesus. God sent an angel to announce to her that, with her consent, she was to become the Mother of His Son. On her answer to this divine invitation depended the coming of Jesus, Who is our joy.

Her consent was awaited by the Most High, and when she spoke her *Fiat*: "Be it done to me according to Thy word" (Luke 1:38), Jesus nestled securely in Mary's virginal womb and, after nine months, was born of her.

"Hail, Mary, full of grace, the Lord is with thee" (Luke 1:28). You pleased the Lord our God, Who chose you for the Mother of His Son, Who is our joy. We hail you, O most sweet and loving Mother, as the Cause of Our Joy. All generations, throughout the endless ages, shall call you blessed.

CHAPTER XXIV
Spiritual Vessel

In the Acts of the Apostles we find a narrative of the life and mission of Saint Paul.

Saul of Tarsus, which was his name before he became an apostle, was a violent persecutor of the followers of Christ. While on his way to Damascus, thinking only of threats and slaughter against the disciples of the Lord, Jesus appeared before him, surrounded by light. He chided Saul for persecuting Him. The light of our Lord blinded Saul, but his heart was changed and he asked our Lord what He would have him do.

Jesus bade him arise and go into the city, where he would learn what would be expected of him. Jesus then called to His servant Ananias and asked him to find Saul of Tarsus, who was in the house of Judas. Once he found him, Ananias was to restore his eyesight, to instruct and to baptize him.

Ananias, who had heard of the persecutions waged by Saul against the Saints of God in Jerusalem, feared him. But our Lord said to him: "Go thy way, for this man is to Me a vessel of election, to carry My name before the Gentiles, and kings, and the children of Israel" (Acts 9:15).

Encouraged by the words of Jesus, Ananias went to the house where Saul was and told him of the mission Jesus had given him.

Saul received him kindly, listened attentively to his instructions and was baptized. His sight was restored and immediately he went forth to preach Christ crucified in the synagogues, declaring Him to be the Son of the living God.

God prepares His servants and gives them the needed

graces for the work He calls them to do in His name. In a miraculous manner He selected Saint Paul, making him a vessel of election, "to carry His name before the Gentiles, and kings, and the children of Israel."

If God condescended to make use of the marvelous to transform Saul the persecutor into Saint Paul the Apostle, who was to bear His name to the Gentiles and proclaim that Christ is the true Son of God, what prodigy will He not be pleased to work in order to create a vessel worthy to carry, not merely His name, but His very Self to the whole world?

The vessel that is to carry Him must be as much like Him as is possible, for nothing less would be a fitting place for Him. But God is an infinite, pure spirit. He is the Alpha and Omega of all things. "I AM," He says, "who am." Saint Thomas calls Him "a pure act." Saint John says: "God is a spirit, and they that adore Him, must adore Him in spirit and in truth" (John 4:24).

In the secrets of Divine Providence, He resolved to take unto Himself our human nature. To do so, He prepared a vessel, all spiritual, wherein He might be carried. He would even take of its matter to form for Himself a body and become man. This spiritual vessel, the wonder of God's creation, was Mary, His Mother, whom He created without spot or stain, immaculate and full of grace.

He put forth the might of His arm in creating her, making her all fair in body and soul. From all eternity, He had chosen her to be the most pure Mother of Jesus. She is that Spiritual Vessel wherein He, the infinite, pure spirit, was carried without compromising His infinite perfection.

CHAPTER XXV
Vessel of Honor

"The Lord knows who are His, and not one of them shall perish."(2 Tim. 2:19) In Saint Paul's Second Epistle to Timothy, he assures his disciple that he is consoled in the fact that God's eternal decree, upon which rests the salvation of His chosen ones, is irrevocable.

Saint Paul continues, "Let everyone depart from iniquity who names the name of the Lord," and he shall be saved.

So why are there many unworthy members in His Church? The Church is likened to a family, whose members differ widely among themselves. "In a great house there are not only vessels of gold and silver, but also of wood and earth; and some, indeed, unto honor, but some unto dishonor." (2 Tim. 2:20)

"If any man, therefore, shall cleanse himself from these, he shall be a vessel unto honor, sanctified and profitable to the Lord, prepared unto every good work" (2 Tim. 2:21). On the other hand, those who follow false teachings, or who surrender themselves to vice, are like vessels of dishonor in the house of God. The vessel of dishonor is not "His" and therefore "shall perish."

Sanctification is the first requisite for the vessel of honor. The more sanctified this vessel, the more precious it is. Of all the members of God's household, in a word, of all His creatures, Mary is the nearest and dearest to Him, because she is the most sanctified. Through her blessed maternity, the Virgin Mary enjoys the closest union that can possibly exist between the Creator and one of His creatures. It was made possible by the loveliness and holiness of the vessel, the immaculate Virgin Mary. She obeyed the command of Zachariah, the father of Saint John the Baptist that we serve God, "in holiness and justice, all our days" (Luke 1:75). She well understood what her Divine Son meant when replying to the woman who exclaimed: "Blessed is the womb that bore Thee." Jesus said, "Yea, rather, blessed are they who hear the word of God, and keep it" (Luke 11:28).

Sanctification, in the words of the Apostle, means: "To present our bodies a living sacrifice, holy, pleasing unto God" (Rom. 12:1). Mary did this all the days of her life. And, while sanctified in body and soul, she was also "profitable to the Lord." To her alone is God, so to speak, indebted, for she gave Him of her own substance wherein to form the body of His eternal Son, Jesus.

He was to be the promised Redeemer, hence He had to become man, and this could be brought about only through the most chaste and ever blessed Virgin Mary, the vessel chosen for the greatest honor in the gift of God to man, namely, the honor of being His Mother. She is, in all truth, the vessel of honor. She was "prepared unto every good work." Her whole life was one continuous act of love towards God and her Divine Son, Jesus. God's will was law with her, and she accomplished perfectly every design that God had on her. He had chosen her from all eternity as that Vessel of Honor wherein He was pleased to dwell.

She is holy above all the saints and angels. She is profitable to the Lord more than all His other creatures. She fulfilled His divine will more perfectly than all of them combined. She is the vessel honored by angels and men, exalted and honored by the Creator Himself.

CHAPTER XXVI
Singular Vessel of Devotion

Saint Thomas teaches that devotion comes from devotedness. Devotion is practiced by those who consecrate themselves entirely to the service of God. It involves the cultivation of all the virtues.

In the Book of Proverbs it is said that wisdom is "more precious than all riches; and all things that are desired are not to be compared with her. Length of days is in her right hand, and in her left hand, riches and glory. Her ways are beautiful ways, and all her paths are peaceable. She is a tree of life to them that lay hold on her: and he that shall retain her is blessed" (3:15-18).

True riches, says Saint Bernard, are not gold and silver, but virtues. Job, deprived of all his belongings, seated on a dung-hill, was nevertheless the richest of all his neighbors, because he practiced virtue. "Fear not, my son," said the aged Tobias, "we lead, indeed, a poor life, but we shall have many good things if we fear God, and depart from all sin, and do that which is good" (Tob. 4:23).

Virtue is the image of the beauty that is in God. Through it He makes us like Himself. Through virtue He communicates His beauty and shows forth His splendor. This is especially so in the Word made flesh, Who is the divine mirror of all virtues, and of Him the psalmist says: "Thou art beautiful above the sons of men" (Ps. 44:3).

There are three degrees of virtue. The first is that ordinary virtue, whereby men conform their lives to the laws of God.

The second degree is attained by those who go farther and seek to become more and more like Him. Their virtues

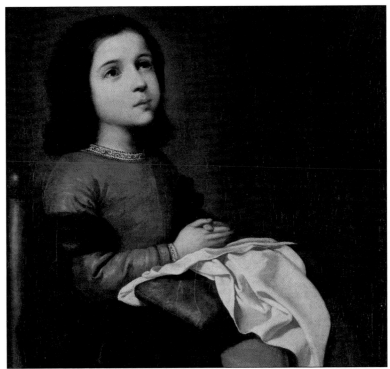

Childhood of the Virgin, (1658-1660) by Francisco de Zurbarán.

are cleansing. By that we mean that by practicing prudence, and meditating on holy subjects, they trample under foot all things earthly and direct their efforts towards the gaining of Heaven. In cultivating temperance they overcome the cravings of the body, and by drawing near to God they are not disturbed by the adversities of life.

The third degree of virtue is still more elevated. It disengages the soul from every attachment to things earthly, and in purifying it, makes it perfect. It is the virtue peculiar to the saints. For whether still in the flesh or enjoying the beatific vision, they are devoted to whatever tends to the honor and glory of God. They sing His praises, they magnify

His name and their mind, heart and soul are aflame with love and devotion for Him.

As star differs from star in brilliancy, so the saints differ from one another in the brightness of their many perfections. The virtues possessed by one are not in the same degree those of another. But there shines out one among them, who, like the sun in the heavens, surpasses them all in devotion, the peerless Virgin Mary.

All virtues and all perfections are to be found in her. From the first moment of her Immaculate Conception, she was more perfect than all the saints united. She had the faith of the Patriarchs, the inspiration of the Prophets, the zeal of the Apostles, the courage and constancy of the Martyrs, the chastity of the Virgins, the purity of the Angels, and the charity of the Seraphim. "Many daughters have gathered together riches: thou hast surpassed them all" (Prov. 31:29). The heavens are not farther removed from the earth than the perfections of the spotless Virgin Mary are above those of all the angels and of all the saints. What can we say of her devotion to the ever Blessed Trinity?

We are as unable to fathom the depths of Mary's virtues as we are to understand the marvels of God's creation. It is a prodigy of God's grace. She, who, from her Immaculate Conception, was full of grace, was singularly devout, loving God and His house among men. Her devotion gained for her privileges denied to all other maidens in the temple of Jerusalem. She alone was given the transcendent glory of being called to be the Virgin Mother of Jesus, the Savior of men.

CHAPTER XXVII
Mystical Rose

The prophet Isaiah, in speaking of the spiritual kingdom of Christ, says: "There shall come forth a rod out of the root of Jesse, and a flower shall rise up out of his root...And the spirit of the Lord shall rest upon him: the spirit of wisdom and of understanding, the spirit of counsel and of fortitude, the spirit of knowledge and of godliness. And he shall be filled with the spirit of the fear of the Lord" (11: 1-3).

In Mary, the Mother of Jesus, is found the verification of those words of the prophet. She is the rod from the root of Jesse, and from it shall bud forth a flower in the person of her Son Jesus, the promised Redeemer. This was why Saint Elizabeth saluted Mary: "Blessed art thou among women and blessed is the fruit of thy womb. And who am I that the Mother of my Lord should come to me?" (Luke 1:42-43).

Saint Elizabeth learned by a supernatural light that Mary was the rod of the root of Jesse, from which would come the flower, her Divine Son, Jesus. Zachariah, her spouse, was also filled with the Holy Spirit and gave forth his prophecy: "Blessed be the Lord God of Israel; because He hath visited and wrought the redemption of His people: and hath raised up a horn of salvation to us, in the house of David, His servant" (Luke 1:68-69).

At the same time, our sweet loving Mother Mary, inspired by the Holy Ghost, Who had overshadowed her, expressed her intense love of God in that ever memorable canticle, the *Magnificat*: "My soul doth magnify the Lord. And my spirit hath rejoiced in God, my Savior. Because He that is mighty, hath done great things to me; and holy is His name" (Luke 1:46-47, 49).

Like the rose among the thorns, Mary, the beautiful "rod of the root of Jesse," grew up among the children of men, increasing in loveliness and fragrance day by day, until, in the words of the psalmist, the "King of Kings greatly desired her beauty." She possessed all the beauty of origin, blood, mind and heart, but, above all, of grace and virtue. Because of her loveliness, God the Father chose her for His daughter, God the Son, for His Mother, and God the Holy Ghost, for His spouse. A closer or more intimate union never existed nor could exist, than that between God and Mary, the rose of His Garden, who grew in the midst of the thorns of trials and sorrows. In His own good time, He transplanted her from the earthly domain into the eternal garden of paradise.

The seven gifts of the Holy Ghost—wisdom, understanding, counsel, fortitude, knowledge, piety and fear of the Lord—filled her soul. They gave her such a profound and pure knowledge of God, together with a new love so intimate that it lost itself in its union with God, as to be, so to speak, transformed into Him. This union, mystical in its nature, was gained by her through the secret action of the Holy Ghost, which is known only to God and Mary, ever Virgin.

Her conception of the Divine Person, our redemption through Him and all the events in the lives of Jesus and Mary are mysteries, known only to God and her. To Mary are attributed the words of the Canticle: "I am the flower of the field" (2:1). She is the fairest of the flowers and she is all beautiful to behold. She is the mystical flower of the root of Jesse. There is none more lovely among all the flowers of the field. She is the rose which is the most fragrant and beautiful of flowers. Connected with the Godhead by the most sacred and closest of unions, her divine maternity, she is honored by Holy Mother Church under the glorious title of Mystical Rose.

CHAPTER XXVIII
Tower of David

In the Canticle of Canticles (Song of Solomon) we have a recital of the blessed union which exists between Christ and His spouse, the Church.

The great mysteries spoken of in the Canticle make special reference to the more perfect souls and especially to the most privileged of all, the Blessed Virgin Mary. Of her Christ says: "Thy neck is as the tower of David, which is built with bulwarks: a thousand bucklers hang upon it, all the armor of valiant men" (Cant. 4:4).

To the modern ear, this praise is a bit odd, at best. It seems the polar opposite of the previous title of Mystical Rose. At first glance it would appear that Mary is being praised for the strength of her body, or her deeds of chivalry, or perhaps her exploits midst clashing forces. But no, Christ speaks of her as the "tower of David ... on which hang a thousand bucklers" because of her power over the enemies of God, in thwarting their evil designs against souls redeemed by the precious blood of her Divine Son.

It is said of her in Genesis, when God spoke to the serpent: "She shall crush thy head" (3:15). Referring to Mary, the psalmist exclaims: "Thou hast broken the heads of the dragon: thou hast given him to be meat for the people of the Ethiopians" (73:14).

In the Canticle, she is spoken of: "Who is she that cometh forth as the morning rising, fair as the moon, bright as the sun, terrible as an army set in array" (6:9).

Commenting upon these words, Saint Bernard remarks, that the demons dread the name and patronage of Mary much more than our enemies fear a great army in battle array. Whenever they find her frequently invoked, they withdraw from their attack, and disappear as the mist before the rising sun.

These words of the Book of Wisdom are applied to Mary: "And being but one, she can do all things: and remaining in herself the same, she renews all things, and through nations conveys herself into holy souls, she makes the friends of God and prophets" (7:27).

Saint Bernardine of Siena, writing on the glories of Mary, says: "All creatures are the servants of Mary, as they are of the Blessed Trinity; for whatever be their rank, whether spiritual like the angels, or human as man, or the elements, whether elect or reprobate, even the demons, all that is subject to God is under the power of the glorious Virgin."

In the Book of Judges it is said of Deborah: "The valiant men ceased, and rested in Israel: until Deborah arose, a mother arose in Israel" (Judg. 5:7). She is a figure of the Blessed Virgin Mary.

In the world, weakness had taken the place of strength. The valiant woman appears in the person of Mary, and through her the human race recovered its lost strength. The mother most pure of Jesus arose in Israel and the demons were put to flight and vices were overcome. Heaven that was shut against man is reopened, and his hope is revived in the redemption of the world through Jesus, the Son of Mary, Virgin and Mother.

Her power did not cease at her entrance into the kingdom of her Divine Son, but now we may liken her to Bathsheba, the mother of King Solomon: "Then Bathsheba came to King Solomon to speak to him for Adonias: and the king arose to meet her, and bowed to her, and sat down upon his throne: and a throne was set for the king's mother, and she sat on his right hand. [...] And the king said to her: My mother ask: for I must not turn away thy face" (3 Kings 2:19-20). Jesus has prepared a throne at His right hand and placed His Mother upon it, where she reigns with Him, the "valiant woman" spoken of in Holy Scripture, "strong with the strength of the King of Heaven, her Son, Jesus."

Another type of Mary, Tower of David, is found in Queen Esther. When King Assuerus saw Queen Esther standing near him, the Scriptures relate that, "she pleased his eyes, and he held out toward her the golden scepter, which he held in his hand: and she drew near and kissed the top of his scepter. And the king said to her: What wilt thou Queen Esther? What is thy request? If you should even ask one half of the kingdom, it shall be given to thee" (Esther 5:2-3).

Santa Maria di Leuca, Leuca, Italy.

In like manner does God, King of Heaven and earth, deal with Mary, the Queen of Heaven and the Queen of earth. She pleases Him; He divides the scepter of His power with her. He refuses no request of hers. She is the most powerful of all God's creatures. She is our defense with Him, our comfort in affliction, and our safeguard against the attacks of the wicked one. She opens up to us the treasures of divine mercy, and Jesus, our Redeemer, is pleased to dispense His graces to us through the prayer of His Virgin Mother, Mary.

CHAPTER XXIX
Tower of Ivory

Our most loving Mother Mary is likened in the Canticle of Canticles to a tower of ivory: "Thy neck is as a tower of ivory" (7:4). In the Book of Wisdom, it is well said of her: "For she is a vapor of the power of God, and a certain pure emanation of the glory of the Almighty God: and, therefore, no defiled thing will come into her. For she is the brightness of eternal light, and the unspotted mirror of God's majesty, and the image of His goodness" (7:25-26).

Mary was always a virgin, therefore, always most pure. Destined to be the Mother of God, it was only right that she should be, after Jesus Christ, the fairest of God's creatures, whether of angels or men.

So pure and chaste is this Virgin of Virgins, that she was concerned about keeping her purity, even to the point of questioning the archangel Gabriel about this. The mission of the messenger of God was to announce to her that she was to be the Mother of the Redeemer. But so jealous was she of her spotless virginity, that were she to lose it, even for such a privilege, she would have declined the honor.

She is truly that "tower of ivory" spoken of in the Canticle, all white, all stainless, "a pure emanation of the glory of the Almighty," into which nothing defiled could enter.

How beautiful are the mountains covered with snow, all pure, that falls from the heavens and covers them in a blanket of untainted white! They glisten like diamonds under the brilliant rays of the sun. How beautiful and white is the silver-like lining of the clouds as they bank in the western sky, when the brilliant sun sinks behind them!

But in nature, purity cannot last. The snows commingle with the tainted elements around them. They become tarnished or melt away under the intense heat of the sun. Every evening the falling shades of night cover in darkness the soft white of the clouds.

How different with an ivory tower! It diminishes not in splendor or whiteness under the bright light of the sun, but shines forth all the brighter, becoming clearer and whiter as the sun's rays fall on it. The rains do not affect it and the heat does not melt it. The more the elements seem to beat down upon it, the firmer and blancher it becomes. It is an image of Mary, and right well is she called the "tower of ivory."

Her purity loses nothing of its beauty by its closeness to the rays of the sun of Eternal Light. Quite the opposite effect occurs. The nearer she approaches the warmth of Eternal Brightness, the more she glows in all her loveliness. All the powers of darkness have not been able to prevail against her. She has overcome their assaults, broken their sway and remains a tower of ivory, beautiful and fair as the morning sun.

Like the "tower of ivory," her purity and strength go hand in hand. The tower of ivory is all white and impregnable. Mary is without spot or stain. She is proof against all the powers of darkness, the ways of a wicked world and the temptations of flesh and blood. She withstands them all; she crushes them beneath her heel while she is seated on her throne, "clothed with the sun, and the moon under her feet, and on her head a crown of twelve stars" (Apoc. 12:1).

CHAPTER XXX
House of Gold

Moses having gone up into the mountain, God spoke to him, saying: "Speak to the children of Israel, that they bring first fruits to Me. Of every man that offers of his own accord, you shall take: gold, and silver, and brass. And they shall make Me a sanctuary, and I will dwell in the midst of them" (Exod. 25:2, 3, 8).

The tabernacle that God wished Moses to build was to contain the Testament which He would give him. It was to be, as it were, the dwelling place of God among His people. From it He would speak to Moses and give him the commands for the children of Israel to follow. Of the metals that were to be used in the making of the sanctuary, gold was to be the most visible. He instructed Moses to overlay the tabernacle with the purest gold both inside and out. In a word, all things ordered for its construction were to be made entirely of gold, or at least they should be overlaid with the purest of it.

This sanctuary was a symbol of the one He determined from all eternity, to make for Himself, a living tabernacle wherein He would truly take up His abode and dwell among us. It was to be none other than His pure, chaste and immaculate Virgin Mother Mary.

If the most precious metals were used in the building of the tabernacle that God commanded Moses to make, how supremely fine and valuable will be the materials He shall select to construct His real, living sanctuary among men! But the beauty of His sanctuary is from within. We shall find it in the exalted virtues that adorned the most pure soul of Mary. So great was her loveliness that she was saluted by the

Angel as: "Hail, full of grace." Because of it, Jesus chose her as His Mother, and the Holy Ghost chose her as His spouse.

God is charity, His Divine Son is the embodiment of charity, and the Holy Ghost is the spirit of charity. How intense must be the virtue of charity in the humble Virgin of Nazareth, who was to shelter Eternal Charity in her!

"If then," writes Saint James, "you fulfill the royal law, according to the Scriptures, thou shalt love thy neighbor as thyself, you do well" (2:8). As the heavens envelop the earth, giving it light, warmth, and fertility, so does charity embrace all, do good to all, lift up, heat, and nourish all. By its sweet and gentle influence, the most stubborn are softened, the most sterile are made fertile.

It is the queen of all other virtues, and is the first law of Jesus Christ, the King of Kings. "Charity is patient, is kind; charity envies not, deals not perversely; is not puffed up; is not ambitious, seeks not her own; is not provoked to anger; thinks no evil. Bears all things, believes all things, endures all things: charity never fails" (1 Cor. 13:4-5, 7-8).

In these praises of charity, the Apostle gives us a true picture of the life of the Blessed Virgin. Out of love for God, she consecrated her entire being to Him. Out of love for God and charity for her neighbor, she condescended to become the Mother of the Man of Sorrows. She watched over Him in the manger; she went with Him into exile; she accompanied Him in His journeys; she suffered with Him during His bitter passion; she stood by Him in the throes of death. Her own soul was pierced by a sword when the heart of that Divine Son was transfixed upon the Cross.

How beautiful is Thy tabernacle, O Lord! How pure, how chaste! How resplendent with virtue! It is overlaid with the purest gold, that charity which "bears all things, endures all things." That "charity" which "never fails."

Mary is the most perfect example of the charity of God. O Mother of divine love, O immaculate Sanctuary of our Redeemer, O living chaste Tabernacle of the Holy Ghost, we hail you as the House of Gold, planned and fashioned by the hand of God for His Sanctuary of Sanctuaries among us. For in you, the "Word was made flesh and dwelt among us."

CHAPTER XXXI
Ark of the Covenant

Saint John tells us in the Apocalypse that "the temple of God was opened in heaven: and the Ark of His Testament was seen in His temple" (11:19).

The Ark of the Covenant seen in the temple of God prefigures the Blessed Virgin Mary. We can draw the following parallels between her and the Ark of the Covenant built by Moses.

The Ark of the Covenant was made of an indestructible wood, while Mary never suffered at any moment of her life the destructive influence of even original sin. The Ark was overlaid inside and out with the purest of gold, and Mary, in her purity, is of the purest of gold. She is so pure that it is said: "All the glory of the king's daughter is within" (Ps. 44:14). The Ark of the Covenant was covered with a mercy seat as a place of atonement; Mary has the power to atone for all who have recourse to her.

Two cherubim, made of gold, spread their wings over the Covenant, whereas choirs of angels hover constantly over Mary. In the Ark were placed the tablets of the commandments; in Mary is the law itself in the person of Jesus Christ.

There was in the Ark the rod of Aaron, which had blossomed; Mary conceived in her womb that incomparable flower of the rod of the root of Jesse. We also find in the Ark a portion of the manna that came down from Heaven and served as food for the Israelites in the desert. In Mary was the Bread of Life that came down from Heaven in the person of Jesus, the Redeemer of the world, who said: "I am the bread of life." "This is the bread that came down from

Notre Dame de la Garde, Marseille, France.

Heaven. Not as your fathers did eat manna, and are dead. He that eats this bread shall live forever" (John 6:35, 59).

The Ark contained the law; Mary, the Gospel. From the Ark came the voice of God; from Mary came the Word of God. The Ark glistened with the purest of gold; Mary shone with the brightness of resplendent virginity. They overlaid the Ark with gold taken from the bowels of the earth, whereas God enriches Mary with the heavenly gold of chastity and charity.

"When you shall see the Ark of the Covenant of the Lord your God, rise you up and follow it" (Josh. 3:3). Behold Mary, the Ark in the temple of God in heaven! We rise up and follow her, paying her homage, respect and veneration.

"The sea saw [the Ark of the Covenant] and fled: the Jordan was turned back" (Ps. 113:3). At the very name of Mary, hell trembles, and the demons take to flight.

Before the Ark the walls of Jericho crumbled. Before Mary the chains that bind the sinner fall from his shackled hands.

The Ark insured victory to the Israelites. Mary obtains for us victory over the powers of darkness, and helps us conquer all our enemies. The Ark of the Covenant was a sign of the presence of God among His people. Mary was the Ark bearing God in her chaste womb, for in her "the Word was made flesh, and dwelt among us" (John 1:14).

The Ark was the guaranty of peace to the Israelites, while Mary contains the "Prince of Peace." The Ark was the power of the people of God; Mary was the tabernacle of the "power of God."

The Ark of the Covenant was the mercy seat of the old law; Mary was that of the new law. The Ark of the Covenant brought the favor of God upon His people and a curse on His enemies. Mary brought blessings to all the human race, but to all who reject the salvation she offers them through the fruit of her womb, Jesus, she brings nothing.

God looked complacently on the Ark, and He takes delight in Mary, His most pure, most chaste, Virgin Mother.

CHAPTER XXXII
Gate of Heaven

In the disobedience of Adam, mankind suffered a serious loss. Adam, and through him all men and nations, was driven out of the Garden of Eden. The gate of the heavenly paradise was closed against him. Though created for Heaven, he sacrificed his claim to it by disobeying the command of his Creator when he ate of the forbidden fruit. His descendants were condemned to the same punishment, and all generations of men found the gate to the kingdom of Heaven shut against them.

Before expelling man from the garden of paradise, God gave him the promise of a Redeemer who would reestablish him in the rights to his heavenly home, would bring back blessing to an earth cursed by his sin, and would reconcile him to his Creator in the shedding of His blood.

The Savior promised by the Almighty was to be born of a woman. God spoke thus to the serpent: "I will put enmities between thee and the woman, [between] thy seed and her seed: she shall crush thy head, and thou shalt lie in wait for her heel" (Gen. 3:15).

A woman was to be the mother of the Redeemer.

No one could enter into heaven until the coming of the Savior. After conquering sin and death, He would return triumphant into heaven in order to reopen it to the children of Adam, who would benefit from His gift of redemption by loving and serving God faithfully.

But what privileged woman was to be the Mother of Him Who would liberate mankind? Since, by sin, Heaven was lost, it can be recovered by perfect innocence only, and an adequate apology made to the justice of an outraged God.

Heaven alone can provide a Savior, while the woman must open the way, be the gate, so to speak, through which He may come to earth in the fullness of time according to the secret designs of God.

That blessed among women was none other than the Immaculate Mary, the Mother of Jesus. By a special privilege of Divine Providence she was preserved from the original stain of Adam through the foreseen merits of the passion and death of her Divine Son, the promised Redeemer. She is truly the gate by which Christ Jesus entered into the world, to do the will of His Father.

Jacob, the son of Isaac, having received his aged father's blessing went into Mesopotamia of Syria. On his way he rested and slumbered. In his sleep he saw a ladder which rested upon the earth, while the top of it reached the heavens. Angels of God came down and returned upon it. And he heard the Lord God of Abraham say to him: "In thee and thy seed all the tribes of the earth shall be blessed" (Gen. 28:14). On awakening, Jacob said: "This is no other but the gate of Heaven" (28:17).

Not in sleep, but while contemplating God, did Mary see an angel descending from Heaven. This angel told her that she was found pleasing to the Lord her God because she was full of grace. He also proclaimed that she was chosen from all women to be the Mother of One through Whom all the peoples of the earth are to be blessed.

He waits for her consent. She must open the way and allow the Just One to come into the world, for she "is no other than the gate of Heaven."

Speak! Oh Mary, speak the word and let the gate of Heaven stand wide open! She spoke it: "Behold the handmaid of the Lord, be it done to me according to Thy word." The gate was opened and the Emmanuel came unto us.

Arising from prayer, she traveled to the home of her cousin, Saint Elizabeth, who greeted her as she entered her home: "Blessed art thou among women, and blessed is the fruit of thy womb [Jesus] ... and who am I that the Mother of my Lord should come to me?" (Luke 1:42-43). Then Mary burst forth in that inspired song of praise: "My soul doth magnify the Lord," and "all generations shall call me blessed" (Luke 1:46, 48). Truly all the generations of men and all the choirs of angels will proclaim her blessed, who "is no other than the Gate of Heaven," the Virgin of Virgins, the Mother immaculate of the promised Redeemer.

CHAPTER XXXIII
Morning Star

"A star shall rise out of Jacob" (Num. 24:17). This star of Jacob prefigures the Blessed Virgin Mary. She is born into the world as fair as the moon, as bright as the sun, and is like the morning star that forecasts the rising of the Sun of Eternity.

Unaware of the star that was to rise out of Jacob, the world slumbered while from out of the heavens came an archangel to announce its appearance and admire it: "Hail, full of grace," spoke the messenger of God to Mary, the humble Virgin of Nazareth. She was heaven's first blessing to earth in the order of redemption.

"Hail, full of grace," without stain, all lovable in the sight of her Creator, rising, as the morning star, of the day, the great day, wherein it would be said, the Savior is born among us.

When Mary was born, the angels of God exclaimed: "Who is she that cometh forth as the morning rising, fair as the moon, bright as the sun, terrible as an army set in array?" (Cant. 6:9).

In creating Mary immaculate, Virgin most pure, Virgin most chaste, God had in mind His Divine Son, who was to be born of her. Her conception and birth foreshadowed the coming of the Savior. She is the morning star of the day of days when He shall be born Who will enlighten every man that comes into the world.

Prior to the coming of the Redeemer, holy souls who were looking for the redemption of Israel sighed and prayed for it, pleading with God to open the Heavens and rain down the just One.

Statue of "Stella Maris" or
Our Lady Star of the Sea.
Church of San Silvestro in
Capite, Rome.

At times, a faint glimmer of hope of the long-awaited-for day appeared on the horizon, and with all the powers of their souls men poured forth prayers of thanksgiving. What would have been their joy had they known that in the birth of Mary, they would perhaps live to see the day wherein the Redeemer would be born?

A dark, dismal night had cast its gloom over the whole earth, which could be dissipated only by the coming of the Savior. Mary was the dawn of that day. "The night is passed, and the day is at hand" (Rom. 13:12). Mary gives us hope, for while she is not the day itself, she is the herald of it.

We cannot see the promised One, but we do behold the splendor of she who is to be His Virgin Mother. She is like the morning star that forecasts the coming of the day so earnestly prayed for.

Eve was the first to give in to the tempter and eat the forbidden fruit. Mary, the new

Eve, is the fruit in the order of redemption. It is she who will thwart the serpent's evil scheme and triumph over him, for she is the immaculate, from whose virginal womb shall come the promised Redeemer who will save His people.

When the Magi came to Jerusalem seeking the newborn king of the Jews, they said: "We have seen His star in the East" (Matt. 2:2). Though all Jerusalem was unconscious of the wonderful happenings at its very doors, a star in the heavens guided those of the East to the manger. They found the child wrapped in swaddling clothes, and falling upon their knees they adored Him.

Saint Elizabeth proclaimed, inspired by the Holy Spirit, "who am I that the Mother of my Lord should come to me?" The great and holy man Simeon proclaimed the same joy, when, in the temple, he received the child Jesus into his arms, saying: "Now Thou dost dismiss Thy servant, O Lord, because my eyes have seen Thy salvation" (Luke 2:29-30).

The night had passed and the day was at hand. The star had risen out of Jacob. The morning star, our sweet, our loving Mother Mary, preceded the great day, wherein the desired of all nations was to make His appearance in the person of Jesus, the Son of the ever glorious Virgin Mary.

CHAPTER XXXIV
Health of the Sick

Since the fall of Adam, misery has become man's portion in life. Adam was told that on whatever day he would eat of the forbidden fruit, he would surely die the death.

Satan, the spirit of evil, was jealous of man's happiness. He therefore led Adam astray convincing him to take of the fruit and eat it. In that hour Adam parted, not only with the beauty of his soul, but he also sustained in his body the consequences of sin.

Sickness, disease and countless infirmities became man's lot. He has now to battle against these ills to prolong a life that otherwise would have endured forever. Man had no hope of getting back all that he lost. God's decree condemning him had gone forth and the "heavens and the earth will pass away," but His word will not pass away.

Man carries in him the seed of suffering and death, because of his disobedience. Having lost the vigor of body and soul, he must have a way to recuperate his strength. Only through constant hard work will he be able to provide for the necessities of life. For his soul, he must seek heaven's sympathy by being faithful to God midst the constantly changing circumstances of his earthly life.

Mankind was promised a Redeemer, who would bring back blessing to the earth and God's friendship to his soul. Yet he must die to resurrect in the last day, provided he loves and serves his Creator during life. The merits earned by Christ on the cross will be applied to his soul to restore health and life to it. In God's own time health will be restored to his body.

As food sustains the life of the body, grace gives life to the

The Divine Shepherdess of Souls by Mariano Bellver y Collazos. Church of the Capuchin Fathers, El Pardo, Madrid, Spain.

soul. When our bodies become weak, we resort to whatever means will reinvigorate them. Every available remedy is sought in order to recover our lost health. If we hear of any skilled physician who has been successful in the treatment of the ailment we suffer with, we quickly seek him out and ask him for a cure.

Man clings to life, parting with it reluctantly. Vast amounts of money are spent by those who can afford it, to prolong their life, even for a short time. If we are willing to do whatever it takes to sustain the life of the body, which will someday return to the dust from which it is made, what should be our zeal in regard to the life of the soul that is immortal?

The eternal life of glory, promised to those who live in the love of God to the end, depends on the health of the soul. "What will it profit a man if he gain the whole world and lose his own soul," or "What shall a man give in exchange for his soul?" (Matt 16:26).

Our greatest efforts should tend to keep our soul healthy. If, unfortunately, it has become weakened by wrongdoing and thereby deprived of grace, which is the life of the soul, we must remedy the harm done by seeking out those means that can heal and restore it to life. If we knew of anyone who could help us in our spiritual frailty, we would be unwise, to say the least, to delay turning to that person.

But Mary, "full of grace," is that one. She has practiced every virtue to the highest degree. Through her the Heavenly Physician of our souls came among us. Therefore it is reasonable to believe that also through her we may find Him in our need. By her humility and admirable purity she brought Jesus Christ from Heaven to earth. She is the Gate of Heaven. By her words, her example and her encouragement, she points the way to Him.

From the cross, Jesus gave her to us as our mother, so that in our trials, difficulties and weakness we may have recourse to her, the best of mothers, and that we may appeal to her in all our necessities.

Were we to attempt to recall all that our blessed Mother Mary has done to restore health to the bodies of the infirm, there would be no end to it. How much more so are we unable to tell all she has done for the health of those sick souls deprived of the grace of God through their own foolishness? Having received the plenitude of grace, Mary comes to the aid of the sick, and the superabundance of grace in her enables them to recover the health of their souls.

She obtains for us all necessary graces for the well-being of our soul. In all our needs we have an inexhaustible source of help in Mary, whose delight is to be the hope of the infirm, the comfort of the distressed, the Health of the Sick.

CHAPTER XXXV
Refuge of Sinners

When sin entered the world, such a scar rested upon it that God conversed no longer with man as He used to do.

There was no place fit for Him. All was dark. Gloom brooded over the earth that the Creator was accustomed to visit before the sin of Adam. In his transgression man closed his heart against his God, Who could find no delight in a place defiled by sin, where He once loved to dwell.

For four thousand years, tears and lamentations marked man's pathway on earth. Deprived of God's presence, all was sorrow, and darkness covered the face of the earth.

From time to time some slight hope entered into the heart of man, when, through rifts in the dense clouds that overspread the world, a faint light from Heaven would come to him. At last the day dawned. From His throne, the Almighty beheld a haven in the person of a humble virgin, where He could find once more an abode among men.

He would descend in the person of His Divine Son into that refuge in which He took delight, become one of us and repair the wrong done by Adam, father of the human race.

No stain of any kind could exist where He chose to find shelter. While He had taken upon Himself the sins of all men, He could not associate with iniquity or seek a refuge where sin was ever known. He is one with His Heavenly Father, Who is eternal holiness, to Whom the very shadow of sin is repulsive.

In Mary—Mary full of grace, Mary most pure, most chaste, Mary immaculate—He found a suitable refuge, where He could enter without offense to His infinite majesty and sanctity. Midst the lilies of Mary's virginal womb the Word was made flesh and dwelt among us.

No sooner was Jesus the Savior born of Mary, than the angels of God announced the glad tidings to the shepherds out in the fields tending their flocks, and bade them to go and find their Lord and God in the manger at Bethlehem. "And they came with haste: and they found Mary and Joseph and the Infant lying in the manger. And the shepherds returned, glorifying and praising God, for all the things they had heard and seen, as it was told unto them" (Luke 2:16, 20).

Protection and salvation had come to them through Mary, and they rejoiced exceedingly that their Redeemer had found a safe place where He was free from the winds and gales of sin.

The Magi, wise men from the East, saw His star in the heavens and journeyed to Jerusalem to find Him, but no trace of Him could be found in that famous city. It was only when they reached the stable at Bethlehem that they found Him through Mary. "They found the Child with Mary, His Mother, and falling down they adored Him" (Matt. 2:11).

The lowly and the great find Jesus through Mary, His only secure refuge.

Man had sinned in Adam, but he longed for the promised Redeemer, Who came to him under the shelter of His Virgin Mother Mary. Only those who looked for Him through Mary were blessed in finding Him, while all who looked for Him elsewhere were unsuccessful and could not find Him.

All men need Jesus and must seek Him, for all have the stain of original sin from their first parents. Those who have strayed further away from God by actual sin, require the saving merits of the Redeemer all the more, so that they may be cleansed of their sins and be restored to His grace and friendship.

The order of things established by Divine Providence has not changed. Hence, to avoid shipwreck on the boisterous sea of life, we must turn toward the Star of the Sea and direct our frail ship toward that secure refuge, where we will be safe from the waves of sin.

We must turn toward Mary, who sheltered Jesus, and who is the refuge to which all sinners may look for safety and salvation in Christ Jesus, Whom they will find through Mary, the secure refuge of sinners.

God honored her in the beginning and He still honors her. He lavished His graces upon her and she faithfully responded to all of them. All who are burdened by sin and far from their true home, should, like the soldier upon the battlefield, who, wounded and bleeding, thinks of his mother, remember their Mother Mary and seek her aid.

She will be their secure refuge and under her benign protection, they will find their merciful Savior. He, like the good shepherd, will place the lost and bruised sheep upon His shoulders and return it to the flock.

The very angels will rejoice because he who was lost has returned and found, through Mary, a safe refuge for all time.

CHAPTER XXXVI
Comforter of the Afflicted

"All ye that pass by the way, attend, and see if there be any sorrow like to my sorrow" (Lam. 1:12).

The prophet Jeremias here laments the misfortune that came upon his people. Having been among them and experienced the afflictions that befell them, he was able to comfort and console them as none other. The heart that has passed through difficulties can be compassionate and encourage those that are being tried more effectively than one that has but little or no experience in the way of suffering.

Intensely applicable are the words of the prophet to the ever Blessed Virgin Mary, the Mother of the Man of Sorrows: "All ye that pass by the way, attend, and see if there be any sorrow like to my sorrow."

Did not the holy man Simeon address her in these words: "Behold this Child ... thy own soul a sword [of sorrow] shall pierce" (Luke 2:34-35). We cannot begin to comprehend the anguish inflicted by this sword that pierced the heart of Mary. It was her Son Whom she had loved more than herself, Who underwent most fearful agonies of body and soul. The same was endured by her through sympathy for her Divine Son, since love is the measure of sorrow.

Christ suffered all His life while on this earth until He gave up His spirit into the hands of His Father on the cross. Mary, His Mother, suffered with Him. And when the Savior cried out in agony from the cross on which He was expiring, "My God, why hast Thou forsaken Me" (Matt. 27:46), the Blessed Virgin, the sorrowful Mother, stood beneath the Cross, breathing forth the same prayer.

Again, the Holy Scriptures give us many points of reference to make sense out of suffering. In the Acts of the Apostles, we find that Saint Paul and Saint Barnabas were zealous in "confirming the souls of the disciples, and exhorting them to continue in the faith: and that through many tribulations we must enter into the kingdom of God" (Acts 14:21).

Statue of the Immaculate Heart of Mary.

The Apostles consoled those who were in distress, pointing out to them that it was by many tribulations they could expect to enter into the Kingdom of God. "For whom the Lord loves, He chastises; and He scourges every one whom He receives" (Heb. 12:6). "For power," Saint Paul tells us, "is made perfect in infirmity. Gladly, therefore, will I glory in my infirmities, that the power of Christ may dwell in me. For which cause I please myself in my infirmities, in reproaches, in necessities, in persecutions, in distresses, for Christ. For when I am weak, then am I powerful" (2 Cor. 12:9-10).

His soul goes out to all who are subjected to trials, sufferings or sorrows, pleading with them to bear patiently their hardships as they see Him do, Who is called on to endure even more than they.

The Apostle consoles them by reminding them of what they may expect: "For I reckon that the sufferings of this time are not worthy to be compared with the glory to come that shall be revealed in us" (Rom. 8:18). "While we look not at the things which are seen, but at the things which are not seen. For the things which are seen are temporal, but the things which are not seen are eternal" (2 Cor. 4:18). He encourages them to be patient under present distresses, and to look forward to what they will bring, the joys of eternity.

In the Old Testament, we read that "the life of man upon earth is a warfare." The holy man, Job, continues "and his days are like the days of a hireling" (Job 7:1). "Man," he adds, "born of a woman, living for a short time, is filled with many miseries" (Job 14:1).

"If I lie down to sleep, I shall say: When shall I arise? And again I shall look for the evening and shall be filled with sorrows even till darkness" (Job 7:4).

In the midst of his greatest afflictions, he sought to comfort those about him and glorify the name of God: "The Lord gave and the Lord hath taken away: as it hath pleased the Lord so is it done: blessed be the name of the Lord" (Job 1:21).

The holy man Tobias, in offering comfort to his people, exclaimed: "Thou art great, O Lord forever, and your kingdom is unto all ages: For You scourge and You save: you lead down to hell, and bring up again."

The Lord "hath chastised us for our iniquities: and He will save us for His own mercy" (Tob. 13:1-2, 5).

How beautiful, how consoling, the words of wisdom spoken by the mother of the Maccabees, who had witnessed the martyrdom of six of her sons. To her youngest son, who was to suffer death also rather than offend God, she said: "My son, have pity upon me that bore you nine months in my womb, and gave you suck three years, and nourished you and brought you up unto this age.

"I beseech you, my son, look upon Heaven and earth and all that is in them: and consider that God made them out of nothing, and mankind also. So you shall not fear this tormentor, but being made a worthy partner with your brothers, receive death, that in that mercy I may receive you again with your brothers" (2 Macc. 7:27-29).

If the holy men and women of God, the Patriarchs, the Prophets, the Saints and Martyrs, tried like gold in the furnace of affliction, were able to comfort and encourage their brothers and sisters in the Faith, what incomparable solace cannot she give to the mournful, who is the Mother of the "Man of Sorrows."

"All ye that pass by the way, attend, and see if there be any sorrow like to my sorrow." Mary, the most perfect of all God's creatures, is loved by Him more than all others, and yet she suffered more bitterly than all the rest.

Her soul was pierced with a sword of sorrow from the moment she offered her Divine Son, the infant Jesus, to God, in the temple. Standing beneath the cross of the Savior on Calvary's mountain, she completed her offering in giving Him as a living victim to the Eternal Father. She offered Him as the clean oblation which was to appease the anger of an outraged God, redeem man and reopen Heaven to him. Having drained the cup of sorrows to the last dregs, she is truly the Comforter of the Afflicted.

CHAPTER XXXVII
Help of Christians

A Christian imitates Jesus Christ, unites himself with Him and lives the life of Christ. A Christian is expected to resemble our Lord; he must be the living image of the Savior, another Christ.

He seeks to resemble God. Adam was made, according to the Holy Scripture, to God's image: "Let us make man to our image and likeness: and God created man to His own image" (Gen. 1:26, 27). Christianity tends to restore man to his first greatness and happiness, to an intimate union with his Creator.

To be a Christian is to be kind to all; to bear patiently with injuries; to help the unfortunate; to be compassionate with those in distress; to share in the sorrows of our neighbors as if they were our own; not to close our door upon the poor; to be deprived of all in the eyes of the world, but rich in the sight of God; to serve and love God with all our mind, with all our strength and with all our heart.

He is a Christian, whose soul is meek and just, whose heart rests in God, and who places all his confidence in Jesus Christ. Whosoever tramples underfoot the things of earth for the glory of Heaven, and despises the world rather than offend God, is a Christian.

As of old, the Israelites were God's chosen people; so today Christians are His chosen people. They were purchased by the precious blood of His Divine Son.

Jesus Christ is their King, and Mary, His Mother, is their Queen. Her interest in them knows no bounds and her assistance is never wanting to them in any of their needs.

Mary Help of Christians, (1868) by Thomaso Lorenzone. Basilica of Maria Auxiliadora, Turin, Italy.

She is a help to them, through her extraordinary example of every virtue. In the midst of the gloom and misery caused by sin, she serves them as the light and the way, to follow in the footsteps of their Savior, pointing out to them that they must take up their cross and follow Him. She teaches the Christian that to love Him is to love all that is good and holy; that separation from Him is misery and death; that to be with Him is happiness and life.

She helps them by her prayers and intercession before the throne of Jesus. She, who is "full of grace," is all-pleasing in the sight of God and most beloved by her Divine Son. At her simple announcement that the wine was running out at the marriage feast of Cana, Jesus was pleased to perform His first public miracle, by changing water into wine. How much more powerful her prayer is now, seated, as she is, on a throne at the right hand of the Savior in the kingdom of Heaven?

He obeyed her on earth. He will not now, in His heavenly home, turn a deaf ear to her pleading for us.

If, by prayer, Queen Esther, in approaching the king, was able to save her people, will not Mary, the Queen of Heaven, in approaching the throne of Jesus and petitioning Him for her people, obtain for them what they humbly ask her to procure from the King of Kings, her most Divine Son?

Mary is the help of Christians, because of her co-operation with the Redeemer in the salvation of the world. She is all beautiful in His sight. She refused Him nothing, gave Him of her own substance, cared for Him and suffered with Him. With Christ she offered His precious blood to God, as a holocaust to appease His wrath and save all men and nations.

Can He now refuse to listen to her prayer on behalf of those for whom He died and who call upon her for assistance? Throughout all the past ages of Christianity we have ample evidence of her help to Christians in times of temptation, distress, wars, pestilence, and all manner of calamities.

She never refuses to come to the help of the poor, the afflicted, the sinner and the saint. All experience her powerful influence at the throne of God. As King Pharaoh sent all who came seeking help in their need to Joseph, so now Jesus graciously grants the help we seek at His hands, through His Mother, Mary, who is also our Mother, and she pleads for us in all our necessities.

She helps us to know Jesus, to serve and to love Him. She helps us to live for Him that we may reign with Him, magnify His holy name and call her "blessed" throughout eternity.

CHAPTER XXXVIII
Queen of Angels

In the Gospel of Saint Matthew we read that: "If a man has a hundred sheep, and one of them should go astray: does he not leave the ninety-nine in the mountains, and go to seek that which is gone astray?" (Matt. 18:12).

It is generally understood that the ninety-nine sheep left in the mountains are the holy angels, who remained faithful to God in Heaven.

The one sheep that went astray is held to be the human race that sinned in Adam. To redeem man, and bring him back to the way of salvation, Christ left the angels, came down from Heaven, and became man. As such He is their Savior, though not their Redeemer.

For the angels He gained grace and glory, election, vocation, all helps and all merit. He is the meritorious cause of all blessings. They had a lively faith in Christ incarnate and were thereby justified.

Mary is the Mother of the Savior of the angels, and, as Queen of Heaven, she is their queen, as well as ours. "The queen stood on Thy right hand, in gilded clothing, surrounded with variety ... And the king shall greatly desire thy beauty" (Ps. 44:10, 12).

The queen spoken of by the Psalmist is Mary. By her divine maternity she became the queen of Heaven and the queen of earth, of angels and of men. All Christians look upon her as their queen, and consider themselves happy to be her subjects.

The dignity of queen is above all other dignities, since it is next to that of the King. The ever blessed Virgin, being

Assumption of the Blessed Mother of God into Heaven, painting by Dias Tavares.

the Queen of Heaven and earth, surpasses in dignity all men and angels. She towers above not only each individual among them in grace, merit and in greatness, but even above all of them united.

The Doctors of the Church teach us that should we place on one side of the balance, all the graces, merits, dignities and glories of men and angels, and on the other, those of Mary, the balance would show a very great preponderance of weight, in favor of the incomparable Queen of the Angels. She is more pleasing to God, more precious in His sight, and more loved by Him than are all His other creatures. Her divine maternity claims for her this privilege. In this capacity she occupies a throne in Heaven beside her Son, Jesus.

A mother is more important than all the servants or children in the household. She commands and they obey. The angels ministered to Mary and were subject to her. They were like ministers bearing messages between her and her Creator.

Saint Gabriel the archangel venerated her, and bowing before her, admired her queenly beauty. From that moment until the angels accompanied her to the throne prepared for her in Heaven, they were subject to her as their queen. "The temple of God was opened in Heaven: and the Ark of His Testament was seen in His temple" (Apoc. 11:19). The Ark of the Testament is Mary. "And a great sign appeared in Heaven: A woman clothed with the sun, and the moon under her feet, and on her head a crown of twelve stars" (Apoc. 12:1).

This woman is the spotless Virgin Mary ascending into Heaven, and taking her place in the eternal mansions of God as the Queen of the Angels. No wonder that all the choirs of angels gave expression to their ecstasy on beholding their queen: "Who is she, that cometh forth as the morning rising, fair as the moon, bright as the sun, terrible as an army set in array?" (Cant. 6:9). Who was it? None other than the Immaculate Virgin Mother of their Savior, their queen.

The Father welcomed her, and presented to her a power due to the Mother of His Son. The Son hailed her coming, and crowned her Queen of Heaven. The Holy Ghost received her, and showered honors upon her, His most chaste spouse. All the choirs of angels and saints of God went before her, and acclaimed her their most pure, most amiable, most loving queen.

CHAPTER XXXIX
Queen of Patriarchs

The Creator was compelled by justice to inflict punishment on man, on account of his sin. Likewise, He was pleased to give him the promise of a Redeemer, in keeping with His infinite mercy.

The first man was commanded to leave the paradise of pleasure God had fitted out for him, repent of his wrong doing, and do penance. Though burdened with many tribulations, which he brought upon himself and his descendants, he lived with the hope that one day his Savior would come, and restore to him the friendship of his Maker.

But Adam was not to live until the coming of the promised Redeemer. Thousands of years were to intervene between his day and that wherein the glad tidings of the coming of the Redeemer would be heralded by the angels, and His star would appear in the East. The promise given to Adam must come down through his descendants to the generations of men, as they would be born into the world. It was the only light of Heaven that glimmered for them through the dark clouds that hovered over them; the only comfort to cheer them on their journey of life; the one hope that held out to them the dawn of brighter days.

The Patriarchs were to be the keepers of the promise for generations. God had chosen these men to be the leaders of His people, and to remind them of the promise made to Adam. They were good, holy men, who feared God and found favor in His sight. To each in turn was committed the custody of God's assurance to man of a Redeemer.

One of these Patriarchs was Jacob. Joseph, his youngest son, had been taken in bondage to Egypt. By his virtue, Joseph had pleased God and became, under the king, ruler over all the land. He then bade his father and brothers to come to Egypt to escape a famine that had broken out at that time. While he was in Egypt, Jacob saw that the time of his death was drawing near. Therefore, he assembled his twelve sons around his bedside to tell them the things that should befall them in the last days.

When Judah's turn came, he said: "The scepter shall not be taken away from Judah, nor a ruler from his thigh, till He come that is to be sent, and He shall be the expectation of the nations" (Gen. 49:10). Referring to these words of the holy Patriarch Jacob, in his allusion to the Redeemer who was to come from the seed of Judah, Saint John says in his Gospel: "Doth not the Scripture say: That Christ cometh of the seed of David, and from Bethlehem, the town where David was?" (John 7:42) Here was David born, and here came into the world its Redeemer, Christ.

The same promise given to Adam in the Garden of Eden was now given to Judah by his father, the great Patriarch, Jacob. The Christ, the Son of Mary, of the seed of David, was the promised Savior. He was the king who should rule over the people of Israel. This would come to pass when the scepter would be lost to the house of Judah.

Mary, the humble handmaid of the Lord, received from the Angel the announcement of the fulfillment of that promise, when she was saluted, "Hail, full of grace, the Lord is with thee." She is the woman whose seed shall crush the head of the serpent according to the promise made to Adam on the threshold of the paradise he had lost. This promise was the only connecting link between Eden and a paradise to be gained through the seed of the great and glorious Virgin

Mary, whose offspring was Jesus, the Redeemer and Savior of the world.

Mary is Queen of the Patriarchs, not only because she became the repository of the promise, but even more because in her it found its fulfillment, as she was from all eternity chosen to be the Virgin Mother of the Redeemer.

CHAPTER XL
Queen of Prophets

From time to time God raised up prophets amongst His people, to keep alive in their hearts the promise of a Redeemer, which He had made to the Patriarchs before them.

The people of Israel were a peculiar, fickle nation. They would serve God for a time; then fall away from Him and stray off into strange, erroneous ways. They often turned from the true God, to the worship of idols. They would complain of the God of Israel and blame Him for the hardships they had to undergo.

By many different calamities He would recall them from their wanderings, have them repent, do penance and be restored to His favor.

No sooner had they been brought back to a sense of duty, then again they would rebel and abandon the service of the only true God, to give themselves over to the worship of false idols. To call them back yet again from their waywardness, God chose at times to send among them His Prophets. He had inspired the prophets to speak to them and warn them of the terrible chastisements that must inevitably come upon them, unless they again turned to Him. The Prophets reminded the people of God's promise of a Redeemer Who would bring blessings again to them. Isaiah tells them: "Behold, I will lay a stone in the foundations of Sion, a tried stone, a corner stone, a precious stone, founded in the foundation" (28:16).

The Prophet here makes reference to the promised Messiah, the Christ, who will come and save His people. Christ referred to this prophecy when He said: "Have you never read in the Scriptures: 'the stone which the builders rejected, the same is become the cornerstone?' By the Lord this has been done; and it is wonderful in our eyes" (Matt. 21:42). The chief priests and Pharisees knew well of whom our Lord spoke, and would have then laid hands upon Him, but they feared the multitudes who looked on Christ as a prophet.

"And thou," says the Prophet Micheas, concerning the birth of Christ in Bethlehem, "Bethlehem Ephrata, art a little one among the thousands of Judah: out of thee shall He come forth unto me, that is to be the ruler in Israel: and His going forth is from the beginning, from the days of eternity" (5:2). The Prophet speaks here of Christ as a man, Who shall rule over Israel. And he speaks of Him as God, for His going forth is eternal. He portrays plainly the promised Redeemer, Jesus Christ, true God and true man.

When the wise men came from the East to Jerusalem to find the newborn King of the Jews, Herod assembled the chief priests and scribes of the people to know of them something about the Christ. Where was He to be born?

They said to him: "In Bethlehem of Judah, for so it is written by the prophet: 'And thou, Bethlehem, in the land of Judah, are not the least of the princes of Judah: for out of thee shall come forth the Captain that shall rule my people Israel'" (Matt. 2:5-6).

The great mission of the Prophets was to turn the people of Israel from their ungodly ways, and keep before them the promise of the Messiah, Who was to be born from among them. But Mary also prophesied. And in dignity, in rank, in the magnitude of her prophecy, she is the Queen of Prophets.

Inspired by the Holy Spirit of truth, after she had conceived the Savior in her womb, she bursts forth in that grand anthem, the *Magnificat*, wherein she proclaims that "all generations shall call me blessed" (Luke 1:48). All peoples and places bear testimony to this prophecy. The churches, chapels, monuments, altars, religious orders and congregations instituted in her honor, confirm it. The prayers, supplications, chants and pilgrimages to her shrines of the faithful throughout the world, to obtain her intercession, proclaim it.

She is more invoked and honored than all the angels and saints combined. To her alone is given the "hyperdulia cult," namely, the special veneration due to the Blessed Virgin Mary. It is substantially less than the adoration which is due to God alone. But it is higher than the veneration due to the angels and other saints.

On the seas, in the valleys, on the mountains, prayers are offered to her. The generations bless her and will magnify her name forever, because of her many virtues: her virginity, her humility, her obedience, her patience, her holiness, her power, her beauty, her mercy, the favors she obtains for her servants, the miracles that are wrought through her intercession, her purity, her divine maternity.

Veneration for her will last, as long as there are men, angels and her Divine Son to pay it to her, as long as God shall be God, throughout all eternity.

She was an object of prophecy, and great among the Prophets, by reason of her own prophecy. She is the mother of the Inspiration of Prophets, the Queen of Prophets.

CHAPTER XLI
Queen of Apostles

The Patriarchs followed their forefathers into death, the Prophets likewise passed into the home of their eternity. Both in their day and generation fulfilled well the mission given them by the Almighty. They were His special servants among men, preserving and handing down to succeeding generations the comforting promise of a Messiah.

Then the great day dawned, and the Redeemer was born into the world. The promise was accomplished. The humble Virgin Mary of Nazareth was the chosen one among women, by reason of her purity, to become the Mother of the "Word made flesh." He is the way, the truth and the life of the world, its promised Redeemer.

Mary carried Him for nine months in her chaste womb, gave birth to Him, and cared for Him through the years of His infancy, childhood and young manhood. She presented Him to the world as the God-man: the Savior foretold by the patriarchs and the prophets. She took Him to the temple, for the rite of circumcision, as required by law for all male children. She made Him known as God, when, at the marriage feast of Cana, He changed water into wine at her request. She was the first to declare to men and nations, to Jew and Gentile, that her Son, Jesus, was the Christ, the Son of God, true God and true man.

Thereafter, Christ went about doing good everywhere, preaching the glad tidings He had brought down from Heaven, and working miracles. To continue His mission among the nations, He commissioned His Apostles to teach all peoples, that He is in very truth the promised Redeemer.

The twelve Patriarchs were the fathers of the Jewish nation; the twelve Apostles were the spiritual fathers of the Christian people. It is also held by Saint Thomas that the number of the Apostles corresponded to the twelve stars that formed the crown that rested upon the head of the spouse spoken of in the Apocalypse, that is, of Mary.

Christ selected His Apostles from among the poor and illiterate, to make it clear that God Himself was the source of their power and knowledge. "For God," says Saint Paul, "has chosen the foolish things of the world, that He may confound the wise, and the weak things of the world has God chosen that He may confound the strong. And the base things of the world, and the things that are contemptible, hath God chosen, and things that are not, that He might bring to naught, things that are. That no flesh should glory in His sight" (1 Cor. 1:27, 28, 29).

The world glories in its wisdom, power and honor, while God selects those considered less wise in the eyes of the world. God uses the less powerful as His instruments, so that the world may know that the work done is a divine work.

The Apostles lived modestly. They neither desired nor sought earthly goods, they possessed nothing. They died to all around them to live for God alone.

Such was the life of Mary in a sublime degree. Looking to Mary as their Queen, the Apostles mirrored their lives upon hers. She passed her days in comparative seclusion, as poor as the poorest, satisfied with her close union with God in prayer and contemplation. The Apostles lived not for themselves, but they lived and died for Christ, who first gave His life for them.

Mary lived for Jesus, and died of pure love for Him. The

Apostles lived and died for the good of souls. Mary's life was one of sacrifice and love for the redemption of men. Isaiah, seeing the Apostles through the light of divine revelation, spoke of them in transports of joy: "How beautiful upon the mountains are the feet of him that brings good tidings, and that preaches peace: of him that shows forth good, that preaches salvation, that says to Sion, your God shall reign!" (52:7).

Mary was the Virgin Mother of Jesus, the reservoir of eternal truth, the spouse of the Holy Ghost and the constant companion of the Man of Sorrows. The Apostles were the ministers of Jesus Christ, the defenders of truth, the mouthpieces of the Holy Ghost, the messengers of the Word of God. They went everywhere, preaching Christ and Him crucified. Of the Apostles the words of Ecclesiasticus may be truly spoken: "These were men of mercy, whose godly deeds have not failed" (Ecclus. 44:10).

Mary is the Mother of mercy and the dispenser of the graces that flow from the seat of mercy. Her deeds of godliness never subside, they are in our own times the admiration of the people of God.

For years after the ascension of Jesus into Heaven, our Lady remained with the Apostles. They were continually helped by her prayers, and led onward to noble deeds by her admirable example. They were bowed in grief when they laid the body of their queen in the tomb, where it was to remain but a few days. It was soon taken into Heaven to enjoy for all eternity the beatific vision. There Mary welcomed the Apostles at their death, into the kingdom of her Son, their Divine Master.

CHAPTER XLII
Queen of Martyrs

The great Doctor of the Church, Saint Jerome, declares that the shedding of one's blood for Christ and His Church is not the only means of acquiring martyrdom, but that a perfect submission to the mind and will of God deserves the same name.

It is not given to all to be called to shed their blood for the faith. But all may merit the title of "martyr," who bend their neck beneath the spiritual sword in overcoming the temptations of flesh and blood that arise in them.

To possess riches, yet be detached from all worldly goods as Job and David; to give bountifully of what we have, like Tobias or the widow of the Gospel; to preserve chastity in youth, as Joseph in Egypt, is to be worthy of the name of martyr.

The holy man, Simeon, told Mary that a sword would pierce her heart: "Thy own soul a sword shall pierce" (Luke 2:35). Mary participated in the coming of the Redeemer into the world, freely giving her consent to become His Mother. In the same spirit of love she agreed to share in all the sufferings and death that God, in His infinite justice, would inflict upon her Divine Son, our Savior, Who took upon His own shoulders the sins of the world.

Mary loved Jesus with a love that surpassed the love of all angels and men for Him. Her love for Him was that of a mother's heart for her son. She loved Him more than herself, and would rather have suffered and died in His stead than see Him bear the humiliations to which His enemies subjected Him.

Christ endured the most fearful agonies in His body. All of these sufferings Mary shared through her sympathy for Him. She knew that our Lord was the Son of God, as well as her own Son in the flesh, which knowledge intensified the anguish of her soul.

The bitter sufferings of Christ and of His Mother were not of short duration, but they began with His entry into life, and cease only with His death upon the Cross.

Mary Most Sorrowful could have exclaimed the same words spoken by her Son as He hung upon the Cross, abandoned by all, "My God! My God! Why hast Thou forsaken me?" (Mark 15:34). If God had not, for His own divine purposes, sustained her, she would have given up her soul into His hands, as the words fell from the lips of Jesus: "Father, into your hands I commend My spirit" (Luke 23:46). As the Savior, in His death and passion, suffered greater torments than all the martyrs, so did His Mother, because of the depth of her maternal love for Him.

In sorrowful Mary, standing upright beneath the Cross, the martyrs of all times behold their prototype in patience, suffering, fortitude, courage, virtue, the love of God, and the sacrifice of their life for Christ's sake. The sufferings of the martyrs, in comparison to hers, are no more than a spring to a great river, or a rivulet to a vast ocean.

The halo of martyrdom that encircles her fair brow gives luster to the crowns of all other martyrs. She is the first, the fairest, the greatest, the Queen of Martyrs.

CHAPTER XLIII
Queen of Confessors

It is an easy matter to follow the leadership of one who is victorious over all his enemies; whose prestige is everywhere hailed with acclamation; who receives homage without stint from his devotees, and who in turn is able to reward them richly for their loyalty to him.

On the other hand, it requires courage, virtue, even the strongest attachment and love to champion the leadership of one who is shorn of all worldly pomp and influence; who has neither gold nor silver to offer; who can bestow no honors on those who organize themselves around his standard.

Such a one is Christ Jesus. He holds out to His followers no earthly consideration—only insults, chains, prisons, hunger, thirst and all manner of persecution. What He does promise, however, is a reward, a crown of glory beyond the grave that no man can take from them.

He offers nothing of this world's goods, nothing of riches, honor, or greatness, but pledges in lieu of the passing pleasures of this life, that which the "eye has not seen, nor ear heard, neither has it entered into the heart of man, what things God has prepared for them that love Him." (1 Cor. 2:9). These are the gifts that Christ gives to those who are not ashamed of Him before man, but confess openly that they are followers of the humble Nazarene.

These "confessors" of the Faith are those brave champions who have confessed Christ publicly in time of persecution and have been punished with imprisonment, torture, exile, or labor, remaining faithful in their confession until the end of their lives.

They are the strength of the Church, the foundation stones of the edifice. They are as pillars of safety against sin and iniquity, or, like pilots who guide the world in the path of justice and truth. They are the true shepherds of souls, who drive the wolves from the flock in their care. They are the laborers who are diligent in ridding their master's fields of weeds of every kind. They are faithful soldiers of the Crucified, who battle against the enemies of God to save souls from ruin.

They are noble victors, having triumphed over the devil, the world and the flesh. They are the champions of the Cross which they hold up high, of which they are not ashamed. They proclaim Christ in Whom they glory, and His word, which they proclaim fearlessly to all men and nations in the face of dangers, insults, imprisonment and persecution. They are the trumpet of the Gospel, the powerful voice of the teachings of Christ, the guides of the people, the upholders of the faith, the depositories of the mysteries of Jesus Christ, the temples of the Holy Ghost.

To these valiant confessors of the faith our Lord said: "You shall be witnesses unto Me, even to the farthest part of the earth" (Acts 1:8). Carry My name before men and nations without fear. "Blessed are ye when they shall revile you, and persecute you, and speak all that is evil against you, untruly, for My sake: Be glad and rejoice, for your reward is very great in Heaven" (Matt. 5:11-12).

The reward He promises is not of this world, but of that which is to come. They will suffer here, but will rejoice hereafter.

Mary confessed Christ before the world. She did this from the moment she gave her consent to become His Mother until standing firm on Calvary beneath His cross. She confessed before Jew and Gentile in her silent and dignified demeanor that the Crucified was the Son of the Most High and her own Divine Son, true God and true man.

In the face of all the indignities offered to Him, she clung to Him. She followed Him through His bitter passion, she walked with Him to Calvary, she received His limp body into her arms, and pressed tenderly to her Mother's bosom that Son, Who so often in childhood rested upon it.

Every insult flung at Him was aimed at her, every humiliation suffered by Him was shared by her. Every blow that fell upon Him, pained her. The nails that pierced His hands and feet wounded her soul, and, when His side was pierced with a lance, a sword of sorrow passed through her heart.

Encouraged by Mary's example, the confessors of the faith will always proclaim Christ as their God and their Redeemer, notwithstanding the blasphemies and insults heaped upon them by the enemies of Christ and His Church.

Mary stood by the standard of Christ. They, following her leadership, cling to it in life and in death. And while they confess and do not deny that He Who died upon the cross is their God and King, they confess and proclaim that she who stood sorrowful beneath that same cross is His Mother and their Queen.

CHAPTER XLIV
Queen of Virgins

"The Queen stood on thy right hand. After her shall virgins be brought to the king: her neighbors shall be brought to Thee. They shall be brought with gladness and rejoicing; they shall be brought into the temple of the king.

"They shall remember thy name throughout all generations. Therefore shall people praise thee forever; yea, forever and ever" (Ps. 44:10, 15-16, 18).

Mary ever Virgin is seated at the right hand of her Divine Son in His heavenly kingdom. As Queen of Heaven, she occupies the place of honor next to the King. This Virgin of Virgins shall lead other virgins to the King, Who, with gladness and rejoicing, shall form His special court. "They are virgins, these follow the Lamb wherever he goes" (Apoc. 14:4).

To them the Psalmist promises the empire of the world. They hold the first rank in the hierarchy of the saints. Because of their voluntary renouncement of all earthly goods and pleasures, which pass like clouds before the wind, they are raised above the other creatures of God. Of Mary, the peerless Virgin, the words of Tobias are spoken: "Thou shalt rejoice in thy children, because they shall all be blessed, and shall be gathered together to the Lord" (Tob. 13:17).

In this quote from Holy Scripture, special reference is made to those who devote themselves to God and spend their lives in the sanctification of their souls in holy religion. Saint Jerome explains beautifully the dignity of those children of Mary, the Queen of Virgins, when he says: "Death came through Eve, life by Mary. She formed a new family, one of virgins, in order that her Son, the King, Who was worshiped in Heaven by angels, might have also on earth, in virgins, angels, who would pay him homage."

Mary was the first among women to consecrate herself to God freely by the vow of perpetual virginity. She has drawn millions of other virgins of every rank, age and condition in life to follow her leadership and live the life of angels among men. They praise and magnify the name of their model and queen, Mary ever Virgin.

They surpass in merit the heavenly spirits, for they are virgins in a physical body, which makes their practice of purity more heroic, and thereby all the more meritorious. They wear a double crown, that of virgin and that of martyr, for the Fathers of the Church assure us that the preservation of virginity is a prolonged martyrdom which will receive a like reward with that of a bloody martyrdom.

"These follow the Lamb whithersoever He goes. For they are without spot before the throne of God" (Apoc. 14:4, 5). In following the Lamb, they follow in the footsteps of Mary, the ever glorious Virgin Mother of the King, and she is always seated at His right hand.

How fruitful is Mary's loving vow of perpetual virginity! She has been blessed with innumerable children who have chosen her as their Queen! They love her virginity and willingly give up all of life's fleeting pleasures in order to follow the Lamb throughout the mansions of His heavenly kingdom.

"All the Angels and Archangels, the Thrones and Principalities, serve you faithfully, O Mary," exclaims Saint Bonaventure. "All the Powers and Virtues obey you; all the Dominations wait upon you; all the Cherubim and Seraphim form your entourage and minister unto you. All the angels cease not to cry out, Holy, holy, holy, is the Mother of God, Mother and Virgin" (Speculi).

The army of virgins enthusiastically joins its voice to the glad chorus of the angels, praising and magnifying the name of their Queen, Mary undefiled, immaculate Virgin of Virgins.

CHAPTER XLV
Queen of All Saints

"Be ye therefore perfect, as also your Heavenly Father is perfect" (Matt. 5:48).

God Himself, according to the words of the Evangelist, is the great model of sanctity. So that we, too, may be saints, He encourages us to imitate Him, to follow His Divine Son, Jesus Christ. "Be ye holy, because I, the Lord your God, am holy" (Lev. 19:2).

Created in the image of God and restored to His friendship through the redemption realized by the Savior, we should have God constantly before us, and aim to cultivate, as far as is in our power, His holiness.

To be a saint is to live in conformity to the will of God. His will being one with His divine spirit, it is necessarily harmonious to the eternal law that governs all things. This same law establishes the measure and rule of all sanctity. In God this conformity is infinite, hence His holiness is infinite.

Sanctity is the love of God and a close union with Him, Who Himself is the fullness of sanctity. In serving God with all the powers of mind, heart and soul we approach daily closer to Him, and become more like Him.

"Be you, therefore, perfect, as also your Heavenly Father is perfect." From the moment of the Blessed Virgin's creation, she was possessed of greater virtues, of more intense love for God than all the saints and angels. Her holiness far surpasses their combined sanctity in much the same way as the waters of the ocean surpass those of a mere stream.

"He that is holy, let him be sanctified still" (Apoc. 22:11). "For the lawgiver shall give a blessing; they shall go from

La Virgen de las Cuevas, (1655) by Francisco de Zurbarán.

virtue to virtue, the God of gods shall be seen in Sion" (Ps. 83:8). Who can, considering these words of Revelation and of the Psalmist, fathom the sanctity of the Blessed Virgin Mary, who, in each moment of her long and saintly life, increased in grace and favor before God?

Who, like her, could say with the Apostle: "For to me, to live is Christ" (Phil. 1:21). "And I live, now not I; but Christ lives in me" (Gal. 2:20). Because of the loveliness of her soul, Christ did really dwell in her, for she is the most holy, the most perfect, the queen of all saints and angels.

Noah, Abraham, Isaac, Jacob, Moses, Joshua, all the patriarchs and prophets are venerated; the Apostles, martyrs, confessors, virgins, holy doctors, all the saints of all times and places are held in blessing.

Of Tobias and his family, the Scripture narrates: "All his kindred and all his generation continued in good life, and in holy conversation, so that they were acceptable both to God and to men, and to all that dwelt in the land" (Tob. 14:17).

But who of all these holy men and women is as acceptable and near to God as Mary? Who among them has uttered a prophecy like hers: "All generations shall call me blessed?"

Saint John writes in the Book of Revelation: "I saw a great multitude, which no man could number, of all nations, and tribes, and peoples, and tongues, standing before the throne, and in sight of the Lamb, clothed with white robes, and palms in their hands: And they cried with a loud voice, saying: 'Salvation to our God, who sits upon the throne, and to the Lamb. Benediction, and glory, and wisdom and thanksgiving, honor and power and strength to our God forever and ever'" (Apoc. 7:9-10, 12).

This acclamation of joy will not stop here. The saints will verify the prophecy of their Queen, "all generations shall call me blessed," by singing her praises also and honoring her, the Mother of God, the Mother of their Savior and Redeemer, through whose merits they now enjoy the blessings of Heaven. They shall bless God because He showed the might of His arm in creating immaculate His Virgin Mother, their Queen.

"Benediction, and glory, and wisdom, and thanksgiving, honor and power and strength to our God forever and ever," through Jesus Christ our Lord and His holy Mother, the Queen of the Angels and the Queen of Saints.

CHAPTER XLVI
Queen Conceived Without Sin

The great and glorious Queen of Angels, of patriarchs, of prophets, of Apostles, of martyrs, of confessors, of virgins, of all saints was by a special predilection of the Creator, conceived without sin, immaculate. The illustrious pontiff Pope Pius IX declared this teaching a dogma of the Church on December 6, 1854.

No words could be more appropriate, none more beautiful concerning our most pure Mother Mary, our Queen Immaculate, than those of the apostolic letter of our most Holy Father, Pope Pius IX of holy memory, who proclaimed the doctrine of Mary's Immaculate Conception an article of faith.

From the apostolic brief we learn that God, Whose ways are those of mercy and truth, Whose will is omnipotence itself, Whose wisdom disposes of all things kindly, saw from all eternity the lamentable ruin of the entire human race. God decreed from the beginning of the ages that, by the incarnation of the Word, He would accomplish the original work of His goodness. In order that man, urged to disobedience by the deceit of the evil spirit, should not perish, He chose and prepared from the beginning a mother for His only Son. Taking from her His flesh and blood, He would be born in the blessed fullness of time. He loved her among all creatures with such a love, that He placed in her alone, by a sovereign predilection, all His kindness.

Elevating her above all the angels and saints, He favored her with the abundance of celestial gifts, taken from the divine treasury, in a marvelous manner. Always and entirely

"I am the Immaculate Conception." Statue in the Grotto of the Apparitions, Lourdes, France.

free from all stain of sin, Mary possessed the fullness of innocence and the greatest sanctity that can be conceived outside of God. She possessed these gifts in such a way that no one, except God, can comprehend it.

And, indeed, it was in every way proper that she should always shine forth with the splendors of sanctity. Entirely exempt from the taint even of original sin, she would obtain the most complete victory over the ancient serpent.

Mother Mary, most venerable, was so pleasing to God the Father that He chose to give His only-begotten Son to her: Jesus Christ, conceived in her heart, yet equal to God the Father and Whom He loves as Himself. He chose to give His Son in such a way that He is naturally one and the same common Son of

God the Father, and the Virgin. Mary is truly she whom the Son Himself chose to be His Mother. And it was she and she alone who was chosen as the spouse of the Holy Ghost Who wished that, by His operation, He should be conceived and born, out of whom He Himself proceeds.

The Fathers of the Church have recognized the image of Mary's purity, her integrity possessed free from all stain of sin and all her virtues in the Ark of Noah, which, after being made by God's command, escaped entirely from the general deluge of the whole world. Again, in the ladder of Jacob "that reached from earth to Heaven, on the rungs of which the angels of God ascended and descended, while God Himself rested on the summit of it," (Gen. 28:12) her untarnished innocence and her sanctity were prefigured.

These same Fathers, using the words of the prophets, have likened the venerable Virgin herself to the pure dove, the holy Jerusalem, the sublime throne of God, the ark of sanctification, and the house that Eternal Wisdom built for Himself. Mary is also likened to the queen, who, filled with delights and resting upon her beloved, came forth from the mouth of the Most High, all perfect, all beautiful, all lovable in the sight of God.

Observing that the Blessed Virgin Mary was called "full of grace" by the Angel Gabriel, when he announced to her her incomparable dignity as the Mother of God, the Fathers and ecclesiastical writers have taught that the Mother of God is the seat of all graces and that she is adorned with all the gifts of the Holy Ghost. Still more, she is the treasured dispenser of these gifts. And because she was at no time tainted with sin, she may participate with her Son in the redemption of mankind. She alone merited to hear from the lips of Elizabeth, inspired by the Holy Ghost, "Blessed art thou among women, and blessed is the fruit of thy womb."

It is also their unanimous belief, no less clearly expressed, that the glorious Virgin, in whom He that is all powerful has done great things, shone with such brilliancy in all the heavenly gifts, that she was an indescribable miracle of God, or rather the accumulation of all miracles. Approaching God as closely as it is possible for a created being to do, she is raised to such greatness that the praises of men and angels cannot do justice to her.

In order to bring out more clearly that state of innocence and justice, in which the Mother of God was created, the Fathers of the Church have often not only compared her to Eve before she fell into the snares of the serpent, but more still they place her above Eve, finding a thousand ways to express this superiority.

Eve, indeed, in following the suggestion of the serpent, lost her original innocence and became his slave. The blessed Virgin, on the other hand, far from ever listening to the serpent, overcame his strength and power entirely by the divine virtue which she had received.

Let us all, therefore, with even more devotion and piety, continue to honor and invoke the Mother of God, conceived without original sin. Let all turn with confidence to that sweet Mother of grace and of mercy in all their dangers, their sorrows and their necessities.

There is nothing to dread. There is no reason to lose hope when we walk under the care, patronage and protection of she who, having for us the heart of a mother, and taking upon herself the affair of our salvation, is solicitous for all men and nations.

Having been appointed Queen of Heaven and earth, exalted above all the choirs of angels and all the orders of saints, seated at the right hand of her only Son, Jesus Christ, what she wishes she obtains; she cannot ask in vain.

CHAPTER XLVII
Queen of the Most Holy Rosary

O ur holy mother, the Church, never ceases to look after the good and welfare of all her children. At the sight of any danger she goes to their aid and with the tender heart of a loving mother, offers them her counsel and assistance. The power of God is with her. The counsel, wisdom, understanding and fortitude of the Holy Spirit dwell in her. The promise of her Divine Founder, Jesus Christ, that He would be with her all days even to the end of the world, is proven over and over again.

The teachings and practices of the Church meet the needs of all men and all times. She offers to those who ridicule holy religion the devotion of the Sacred Heart of Jesus. Those who deny original sin, she confronts with the Immaculate Conception of the Blessed Virgin Mary. Upon those who seek only the things of this world, she presses the life of the poor. To those who live lives of ease and impurity, she offers the example of the indefatigable Saint Joseph, the chaste spouse of the Blessed Mother of the Savior. To all she holds up Mary as their help, their support, their secure refuge, rich in every virtue, and blessed with the plenitude of the graces of Heaven.

Many, very many, devotions have Mary for their object. There is one among them that seems to embrace all other acts of piety in her honor, that of the devotion of the Holy Rosary. It originated in France, in the province of Languedoc, in the beginning of the thirteenth century. At this time, great havoc was being wrought in the Church by the revival of an ancient heresy, that of the Albigenses.

Stained glass depicting Our Lady giving the Holy Rosary to Saint Dominic de Guzmán.

Both Church and state united their forces against the common foe, but without success. It was the plan of Divine Providence, for a zealous religious, a true man of God, Saint Dominic, to suppress the disorder, and obtain a signal victory over heresy and irreligion.

Saint Dominic had labored tirelessly to bring those deluded souls back to God, yet little headway was made. He fortified himself over and over again by prayer. One day while the Saint was in fervent recollection, pleading with God to show mercy to the enemies of Christ and His Church, Mary disclosed to him a way that he could triumph over those poor wandering souls and obtain victory for the Church.

"Know, my son," said the Blessed Virgin to him, "that the means which the Adorable Trinity employs for the salvation of this world is in the Angelic Salutation, which is the foundation of the New Testament. If, then, you wish to overcome hardened hearts, preach my rosary."

Without delay, Saint Dominic obeyed the heavenly vision, and, with the rosary as his only weapon, he set out to win for God souls dear to Him and to Mary. This vision of the Blessed Virgin to Saint Dominic was not her first, nor has it been her last to favored souls. Often she has been, so to say, God's angel bearing glad tidings to men of good will, young and old.

The happy results of the preaching of the rosary were marvelous. History places the number of those misguided souls who returned to the one true Faith, at above 100,000 families. A glorious victory for Mary and her rosary.

This, however, was but a glimpse of what the rosary was to win for Christ and His Church in every land and corner of the globe. Today, every devout child of Holy Mother Church clings to his rosary as to his very life, knowing that this devotion has the power that will enable him to overcome the devil, the world and the flesh. Rather than part with his rosary, he would prefer to sacrifice his life, for losing his life in such a cause would be to gain it for all eternity.

It is a devotion pleasing to God and to His most admirable Mother Mary. The "Our Father" was taught to us by our Lord Himself, while the "Hail Mary" comes directly from God through the Angel Gabriel, Saint Elizabeth, and the

Church, inspired by the Holy Ghost.

The rosary contains fifteen decades of "Hail Marys," with one "Our Father," before each decade. It is a brief yet beautiful history of Jesus and Mary, from the moment the angel saluted her, "Hail, full of grace," until she was crowned by the hand of her Divine Son as the Queen of Heaven and the Queen of earth.

The rosary is divided into three parts, each containing five decades. It is known as the chaplet which signifies a wreath of natural flowers worn on the head as a special mark of distinction.

Rosary derives its name from "rose," simply, the queen of flowers, while the "Hail Mary" is called the "queen of prayers."

In praying the rosary we weave the "queen of prayers" into a beautiful crown of Mary's roses, which we place upon her fair, queenly brow and salute her as Queen of the Most Holy Rosary.